D1207325

Tony Greenland's
PANZER MODELLING MASTERCLASS

Tony Greenland's
PANZER MODELLING MASTERCLASS

Tony Greenland

First published in Great Britain in 1996 by Windrow & Greene Ltd

© A.J. Greenland 1995

This edition published in Great Britain in 1999 by Osprey Publishing
Elms Court, Chapel Way, Botley, Oxford, OX2 9LP

ISBN 1 84176 095 1

Designed by Tony Stocks/TS Graphics
Printed in Hong Kong

99 00 01 02 03   10 9 8 7 6 5 4 3 2 1

A CIP catalogue record of this book is available from the British Library

For a catalogue of all books published by Osprey Military, Modelling, Aviation and Automotive please write to:

The Marketing Manager, Osprey Publishing Limited, PO Box 140, Wellingborough, Northants NN8 4ZA, United Kingdom
Email: info@OspreyDirect.co.uk

Osprey Direct USA, PO Box 130, Sterling Heights, MI 48311-0310, USA
Email: info@OspreyDirectUSA.com

OR VISIT OUR WEBSITE AT
http://www.osprey-publishing.co.uk

CONTENTS

ACKNOWLEDGEMENTS & FOREWORD

It was thirteen years ago when I recommenced my modelling hobby after an absence of some twenty-five years. During those thirteen years I have been fortunate enough to achieve a standard of modelling armoured fighting vehicles that has led my publisher to ask me to write this book. I am not wholly responsible for this achievement, and much of my success must be shared with others close to me.

First and foremost is my wife Susana, who has provided constant encouragement and shown unfailing tolerance of my bad moods when models (and more recently, manuscript) have not gone according to plan. She has frequently taken on board those domestic responsibilities which should normally fall to the male, e.g. decorating, bricklaying, etc....Gratitude is also due to my two sons, Andrew and Ian, who spent much of their formative years on their hands and knees, searching the carpet for that lost piece of detail.

Two people have been especially helpful. Lynn Sangster, very much the father figure of military modelling in England, has been consistently kind, generous, enthusiastic and encouraging since we first met a decade ago. I must also record my gratitude to Heiner Duske, who has become a very close friend in the last few years, and who has responded to my limitless requests for information and reference with punctuality, patience and generosity. The plethora of details on my model vehicles invariably owe their origins to information provided by Heiner.

It was a specific request from the publisher that I include a brief section on crew figures. Any observer of the few figures I have painted will realise that this presented me with serious problems. The answer came in the form of Stefan Müller-Herdemertens, a young German artist who has captivated fellow-modellers across Europe with his outstanding figures of many periods, but particularly of Second World War subjects. I cannot thank him enough for his invaluable contribution to this book.

*   *   *

As a small boy, like most of my contemporaries I made plastic kits. In the mid-1950s these were restricted to Airfix models. My favourites were the Tiger and Panther; these two vehicles had a malevolent beauty which I recognised even at that early age, and which I still appreciate today. This early interest in Second World War German vehicles was rekindled some twenty-five years later. I will always be grateful for what I considered the poor quality of British television programming at that time, which drove me to seek another form of evening entertainment. I went to my local hobby shop and bought Tamiya's old Tiger kit; I made it one evening, and painted it the next. I must admit to a very misplaced, if shortlived, sense of achievement. The owner of the hobby shop recommended that I read Shep Paine's book *How to Build Dioramas* ; this quickly put my

first efforts into proper perspective, and the model was given to my one-year-old son to appreciate! (Though now sixteen years old, that book which was my first inspiration remains, in my opinion, a classic.)

Since then, I haven't looked back; and I hope that from plagiarised styles and techniques I have developed for my models a unique appearance and finish. Some people have been kind enough to say that my standards have developed remarkably quickly; I was writing articles within two or three years of commencing the hobby. The reasons are not too difficult to understand.

After giving up modelling when I was ten or eleven my life developed in the usual way. My chosen profession was that of a land surveyor, and in time I developed the skills associated with this vocation - very precise measurement; comprehension of scales and angles; and technical drawing. These skills would form a useful basis for scratch-building and kit conversions many years later.

For the past fifteen years I have been an estimator/programmer in the construction industry. This requires the pricing as accurately as possible of the cheapest and exact cost of any construction project. The reader should understand that this involves limitless permutations, and always to a deadline. How can this be an advantage to a modeller? Well, in estimating it is impossible to be selective with your efforts; the profession demands a consistent approach to all projects. Those schemes that may look unattractive have to be given as much attention as the more favoured projects. Thus, I hope my collection of German vehicles has a consistency of quality, whether a rather mundane little PzKfw I or an elegant Jagdpanther. I cannot deny that making Tigers provides me with my greatest modelling pleasure, but I do try to apply an

even effort to all of my projects.

The other aspect of my professional life that also assists me in my hobby is the constant necessity to programme construction works in the most efficient and cost-effective sequence. This is frequently required in modelling. When you are working from sequenced plans provided with a kit you only need to plan the order of painting; but when undertaking a scratch-build or conversion it is essential to plan the whole construction sequence so that access and availability are maintained. Most people outside the hobby think that modellers have infinite patience; this is certainly far from true in my case, and witnesses will confirm that I hate pausing to wait for items to cure or dry. I therefore try to plan my modelling in such a way that by using different compatible materials, i.e. enamels and acrylics, I am able to model for as long as I want without wasting time.

Once my main hobbies were ornithology and entomology, to which I devoted a large part of my spare time from the age of twelve. I believe I took these pursuits to a reasonably high level; and I was actively involved with formulating the understanding of the problems of recognition of difficult species. Simplifying this science is purely a matter of intense observation of detail. To be able to spot minute differences between species is not totally different from distinguishing between similar marks or makes of vehicles. Being able to spot this sometimes minute detail (while not always understanding its use!), and recreating it on the model, is one of the most important facets of my modelling ethos.

Since I was able to hold a pencil or paintbrush I have always tried to enjoy art. At an early age I decided that while I had some technical ability I had no true artistic talent. I had the technique to reproduce a good likeness of the subject; but frustratingly, I had no original creative imagination. Painting AFVs requires no imagination, only a technical ability to use artists' materials to copy what you observe from reference. Consequently I found far more satisfaction in painting tanks than birds or butterflies.

My last important facet is my interest in history, particularly modern history. To have a full understanding of the chronology of one's subject is as important as some of the technical aspects of the hobby. Those who have an active interest in the history of their subject will certainly be better modellers than those who have none. When I commence modelling a particular vehicle I have already decided not just which version I will reproduce, but also the unit it was attached to, the theatre of operations in which it served, and the year and season. Only by understanding the relationship of vehicle, mark, camouflage, unit and theatre of operation can you produce a model which can be said to be historically accurate. Reading military history of any period, but in particular that of Second World War Germany, gives me enormous pleasure - almost as much as modelling itself.

Put all these facets together and you have my ethos for my modelling hobby. One question I am constantly asked is "Why German ?" This is not easy to answer, especially when one considers the barbarity displayed by sections of the German armed forces. As I lost my grandfather in the First World War and two uncles in the Second my attitude was initially one of reserved neutrality; but studying the history of the Panzer Divisions led me to the opinion that these units were more than worthy opponents of the Allies. Time and time again I read that despite inferiority, both in numbers and equipment, their organisation, training and comradeship showed through and led them to great strategic victories in the first three years, and to many tactical victories in the last three years of the war. It is unfortunate that the Panzer Divisions will be judged by the political system which their military efforts supported. Were it not for the horrendous crimes of the Nazis then I am sure that these troops would enjoy an indisputable place in the annals of military history. I believe it is a British characteristic to acknowledge the military ability of other nations, especially

those who have resoundingly beaten us on the battlefield; this is part of our magnanimity. Also, of course, there is the fact that the endless variety of camouflage and vehicles gives me a hobby with no completion date. If I could produce a new model every week and lived to be a hundred, I would have an ample number of vehicles left to construct.

*   *   *

The hobby of AFV modelling is certainly cyclical. Both Tamiya and Italeri were at their most prolific in the mid-1970s. When I commenced my interest in German AFVs in the early 1980s the hobby was on the wane, with few new kits being produced. At this time Francois Verlinden began his meteoric rise to fame. His dramatic AFV dioramas were the catalyst for the new "cottage industries" which soon proliferated. In the last ten years the needs of the AFV modeller have been well served by these usually small units, hand-producing the requirements of the enthusiast: not only complete models but also a host of accessories, the most important perhaps being the etched brass sets which have added a new dimension to the detailing of vehicles.

However, there was one problem with these individually hand-crafted items: the cost. Whereas modellers were used to paying around ten pounds for their plastic kit, the hand-made resin models were perhaps four or five times this price. These specialist manufacturers catered for the more unusual vehicles and frequently produced a model far superior to that of the large plastic manufacturers. The large manufacturers have recognised this rekindled interest in AFVs, and have once more entered the market (together with one new manufacturer, Dragon). While prices for plastic AFVs were once rather similar, we now have a very substantial difference - which may also be reflected in quality. The re-entry into the market of the large manufacturers will, I believe, bring about the financial demise of the less professional of the smaller companies. This is not a bad thing for the hobby; despite the excellent quality of some of the resin/white metal producers there were many

who did not offer value for money. The limitations of production - whether by industrial scale injection moulding techniques, or by those of the specialist "cottage industry" - mean that etched brass super-detailing sets will be here to stay. Indeed, they are increasingly incorporated within the kits; but specialist accessory manufacturers will, I hope, continue to flourish. The other main area of improvement is in communications, with a substantial number of publications specifically designed for the modeller. Access to museums, both foreign and domestic, is now relatively easy, with even the furthest museums within a few hours' flight time. The 1990s are certainly a golden era for the AFV modeller.

*   *   *

The scale that I work in - 1:35 - is, I believe, the optimum; it provides the most comfortable size for detail work, and for the modeller who wishes to build up a collection it is the scale supported by the main manufacturers. While reference within this book supports that scale, I appreciate that there is an increasing interest in larger scales; while this is not my preference, it will put a greater onus on the modeller to include additional detail precluded by a smaller scale. Equally, while this book describes only German vehicles, most of the disciplines described are equally applicable to any AFV model. The title "Masterclass" (chosen, I hasten to add, by my publisher) supposes that most readers will have reached a certain stage in their modelling careers and will not be total novices. I hope that the contents of this book will appeal right across the spectrum of AFV modellers.

The section on painting insignia would have made little sense without the inclusion of brief reference material on divisional and tactical markings. To those with a deep understanding of this subject I apologise for the brevity of the descriptions; whole books have been written exclusively on this extensive subject, and my objective here is purely to give the reader a good grounding, with reference to where a fuller discussion can be found.

CHAPTER ONE
TOOLS

Just as serious modellers obsessively collect kits, etched sets, accessories etc., most enthusiasts also become prolific collectors of tools. That we rarely use the majority of items already in our toolbox does not seem to occur to us as we happily purchase the next wonderful find - that obvious panacea for all our future modelling problems. It's part of the fun, but on sober reflection a needlessly expensive luxury.

I have tried in this chapter to be realistic about the minimum tool requirements to achieve a good standard of model construction. I will deal firstly with the bare essentials which should enable the average modeller to construct a basic kit and also to super-detail, including all types of kit from plastic to resin and white metal. In order to achieve scratch-builds and conversions the modeller will need additional specialist tools. The list below is not exhaustive nor in any particular order, but purely indicative of my own requirements. (The special techniques of soldering, vacuum-forming and Zimmeriting - all essentials of high quality finishes - are dealt with in Chapter Six.)

Before going into any detail, I would offer one piece of general advice: always buy the best quality tools that you can afford - you will rarely regret it. It is, for example, false economy to believe that Chinese-made needle files, of which you can buy a set for the price of one UMV Swiss file, are going to last as long.

Before you start acquiring your tools and models you will need a regular place to work. The ideal situation is a personalised hobby room where you can spread everything out, and which you can walk away from after a modelling session, to recommence at your leisure, without having to put everything away and then get it all out again. Regrettably I am in the latter position, and have to work on my kitchen table! The main requirement is for a large, flat surface with good light, natural and artificial - and good ventilation. Certain glues and paints have potentially harmful solvents which can be extremely dangerous if inhaled.

This may sound rather ridiculous, but the choice of your carpet may well govern the level of frustration attending your modelling. The comment in the Foreword about my sons spending considerable time on their hands and knees looking for missing bits was not entirely a joke. Do not model over a heavy shag pile carpet; use either linoleum or a short pile. A solid light colour is also preferable; however, deciding the colour of your carpet to meet your modelling needs may require skilled diplomacy with your wife or girlfriend....

Hobby knives

Perhaps the single most important modelling tool is the knife. I use an X-acto holder with *Swan Morton* surgical blades, which come in sealed packets of five for about 60 pence. There are a number of different types, my

personal preference being for the fine-pointed Number 11. Each blade may last for weeks if used for cutting plastic, or only minutes if removing etched brass from the fret. Always use the sharpest blade possible; most problems concerning blades occur because they are blunt, not too sharp. A number of companies now produce saw blades with a variable number of teeth per centimetre, and I find these more suitable and easier to use than conventional hack or fret saws. They fit easily into the X-acto handle.

Files

These tools present the novice with an immediate dilemma, not only over the type but also over the right price to pay; few tools vary so much in quality and price. As mentioned above, needle file sets can be bought for a few pounds; these will invariably be manufactured in the Republic of China, and regrettably have a very limited lifespan. If your interest in the hobby is only slight then perhaps you should consider them. However, after many years all mine are now *UMV Swiss files*; in my opinion these precision tools are the best in the world. A modelling file should be acquired specially for a specific operation in construction, in addition to any ordinary general-purpose files which you may have in the toolbox.

UMV Swiss files are made of chrome alloy steel for extreme hardness and durability. My set of Swiss needle files are approximately 16cm long and include the basic sections - square, rectangular, round and triangular. Good quality files are made with a choice of "cuts", meaning the depth of abrasion removed by filing. The scale goes from 0-6 in graduations of 2, with No.0 the roughest and No.6 a very fine cut. My most frequently used file is called a "pillar" (rectangular section) with a No.0 cut. The other files are either No.2 or No.4 cut, and are used for finishing. Sometimes the modeller needs to file in inaccessible locations, and the solution is to use "riffler" files. These uniquely shaped curve-ended files allow easy access; once again, a variety of sections of these usually double-ended files are available. My last essentials are specifically called "miniature

files"; these are 50mm long and approximately 1mm in diameter, tapering to a very fine point. Manufactured in round and square sections, these beautiful miniature tools are perfect for enlarging very small holes or for putting in a 90 degree corner.

Files can quickly get clogged with white metal, resin or plastic detritus, and are best cleaned with a brass wire brush. When using the smaller files great care should be taken - these are delicate instruments, and worth cherishing.

Tweezers and scissors

You will need both these tools, and I can only repeat that you should buy the best you can afford. Apart from one or two conventional pairs for general purpose work I have one pair of very expensive *Taxal* tweezers, made from a vacuum treated alloy of chromium, cobalt and titanium, which gives 100% protection against corrosion. They are non-magnetic, and unaffected by heat up to 500 degrees C. Most enthusiasts will appreciate these qualities: how many times have we lost the hardness of tweezer tips by holding detail parts while soldering?

Scissors I do not use a great deal, but I have one good quality general purpose pair which are strong enough to cut thin brass/copper sheets. I do occasionally use nail scissors for cutting fine brass or plastic sheet to a given radius.

Pliers

Given the increasing use of etched brass and my own preference for working in metal, I have a small number of quality pliers and cutters. I use *NSD* box joint pliers/cutters; designed specifically for pressure work, they retain precise alignment even under strain and considerable use. When deburring or shaping fine section metal it is vital that the object is

Above
My tool box (deliberately tidied for the photograph...) contains 90% of the tools I use on a regular basis. Replacing tools in their correct compartment saves wasting valuable modelling time in searching for them.

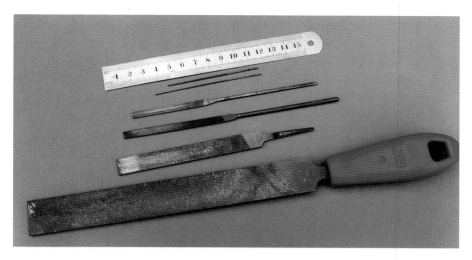

Above
A selection of the files which I regularly use; do not be afraid to use a large, coarse-cut file when appropriate. The files nearest the rule are miniature "needle files" for fine work and finishing; delicate and expensive, these are worth the cost, and will last well if treated with respect.

held tightly in the jaws (so that you do not spend the next half-hour on your hands and knees, peering and cursing). I use snipe nose for the majority of tasks, and a pair of round nose, with either end- or side-cutters for snipping brass/copper rod. Side-cutters are very useful for removing plastic parts from the sprues; they cut cleanly, leaving little need for cleaning the plastic parts. If your hobby shop does not stock them, try your local electricians.

Measuring & calculating tools

If you don't intend to undertake conversions or scratch-builds then the tools you require under this section will be minimal: a 15cm carbon steel stain faced rule, together with a simple calculator, should suffice. The calculator is optional, but a distinct advantage if you want to check the accuracy of a kit. The calculator needs only the four basic functions, plus square root, percentage, memory, and if possible a constant.

If you intend to convert or scratch-build then you will need a sliding calliper gauge, a protractor, a set of two clear set-squares, and a fine point propelling pencil.

Drills, bits & discs

Although it would be possible to construct a manufacturer's kit without a power drill, in my opinion this tool is almost indispensable. I never build straight from the box; the limitations of mass production methods mean that there are always items of detail to add. As I use a variety of materials I need the use of a power tool; work that would take hours to execute by hand can be completed in minutes, and with a better standard of finish.

The exact definition of the tool I use is a miniature electric drill, but the attachments and accessories that I use turn it into a multipurpose power tool. My own is a *Como* drill, costing about £50.00. If you should decide to buy one, the only essential is that your drill must have a speed control. Plastic melts at a low temperature, and the friction heat

generated by a craft tool at fairly low RPM is sufficient. My drill has RPM from 0 to 15000, and I would estimate that 95% of my use is at the lower end of this range - only when cutting/shaping brass do I increase the speed. Before purchasing a drill check that it feels good in your hand, and that the switch is easily accessible; if you have to use your other hand to turn it on and off then the drill is of little use for modelling. Also consider the weight: you will sometimes be holding it for considerable periods at a time.

The available tools and accessories are extensive and will normally fit most drills. My own comes with both a variable chuck, and brass collets of different diameters. Most drills come with a small range of tools. For the modeller, once again the temptation is to purchase every type of accessory available; I would recommend the following as the basic minimum.

A selection of *burrs* are perhaps the most important tools, together with one or two *cylindrical cutters*. All of my brass cutting and

Below
My miniature power drill, an indispensable tool for the serious modeller. Note the variable speed control, essential for work on plastic, which is susceptible to friction heat.

shaping is done with *slitting discs*. These thin (0.6mm) abrasive discs are fitted to a mandrel (holder) by a simple screw; they will cut through any metal, deburr, etc., and they are cheap. This is just as well, as they suffer a high breakage rate, especially after they become worn. Another abrasive, which is not very commonly used but which I find indispensable for cleaning metal, is the *silicon rubber disc*. These "flying saucer-shaped" green rubber discs are impregnated with silicon carbide particles and are perfect for cleaning metal parts and removing excessive solder from joints. Depending on the pressure applied, they can either cut white metal or polish it to a mirror finish. Occasionally I also use abrasive *grinding heads*. Lastly there are, of course, the actual drill bits. In the motor tool I prefer *shanked twist drills*, which have greater strength than ordinary twist drills; however, they are not made in the very smallest sizes.

For delicate drilling, other than in brass, copper etc., I use a *pin vice*. My preference is for a two-way reversible steel type, providing a choice of four different diameter sizes between 0.1mm to 3.0mm.

Metal carvers & spatulas

At most model shows you will find the stalls of hobby tool companies, who frequently offer for sale surplus medical and dental supplies. For bargain prices you can obtain excellent implements, ideal for shaping and moulding a range of pliable materials, e.g. epoxy putty. Should you wish to buy the purpose-made article then you can obtain them from any high quality tool supplier under the title of *wax carvers and spatulas*; a variety of shapes are available.

Consumables:

This term covers here those supplies which the modeller will use on an almost daily basis. I have restricted this to glues, abrasive paper and epoxy fillers.

All models, whether kits, conversions or scratch-builds, and of all materials, need a glue to bind the parts together. I use four types: a plastic solvent, epoxy, cyanoacrylate, and children's white glue.

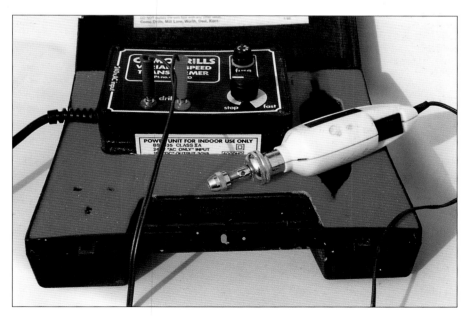

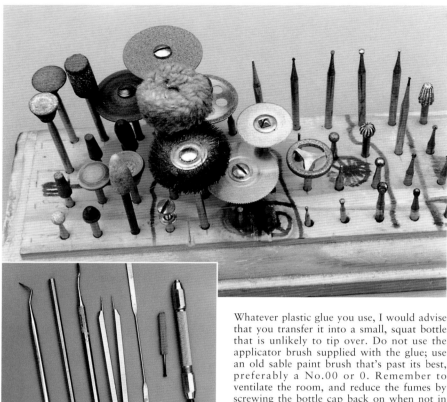

Left
A selection of motor tool accessories. In this photograph the two accessories I use most often are the silicon rubber disc and the slitting disc (top row, third and fourth from left).

Above
A selection of useful tools: from right, a pin vice with up to four different collets; a nail fixed into a wooden handle, for heat-sealing vinyl tracks; various metal carvers and spatulas, ideal for working with Milliput, etc., and a pair of dividers, useful for transferring measurements.

Plastic glue

With plastic kits the most effective glue is liquid plastic cement. This comes in a variety of strengths; regrettably, the stronger, the more dangerous. All plastic cements are solvents which work by dissolving the two surfaces of plastic and welding them together. The thinner and stronger the cement, the better and more successful the bond. If the glue is of the consistency of water you can obtain excellent capillary action - apply the glue in one place and it runs right along the joint. The flow characteristics, while normally a great advantage, do present problems for the clumsy: if your fingers should be on that joint, then you will engrave your fingerprints into the plastic.

I use a very dangerous solvent called MEK, which is a cleaning fluid. Its evaporation rate is phenomenal; used in very small quantities it provides a strong, fast bond for all plastics. The "downside" is its extreme toxicity, and its manufacture will soon cease; I therefore need to find a suitable alternative. The plastic glues found in hobby shops are, to date, a very poor substitute; we must hope that safer and stronger glues will soon be on the market.

Whatever plastic glue you use, I would advise that you transfer it into a small, squat bottle that is unlikely to tip over. Do not use the applicator brush supplied with the glue; use an old sable paint brush that's past its best, preferably a No.00 or 0. Remember to ventilate the room, and reduce the fumes by screwing the bottle cap back on when not in use.

Epoxy glue

These are almost always two-part glues composed of an adhesive and a hardener. You need to mix equal quantities from both tubes; once they are thoroughly mixed you generally have between five and ten minutes before the glue sets. A further 24 hours is needed to fully cure and harden. It is very messy glue, which tends to string once mixed and is difficult to apply in small quantities. Good points are its great strength and long working time. Use this, for example, for attaching white metal/resin wheels, where the bond may tend to distort under the weight of the vehicle.

Cyanoacrylate

Known more commonly as "super-glue", this adhesive has made a dramatic improvement to the quality of kit presentation. Without getting too technical, a chemical reaction takes place when the ethyl cyanoacrylate comes into contact with water vapour. This action causes the glue to change from a liquid state to solid. Water vapour is found on virtually all objects, hence super-glue's amazing ability to stick virtually anything. Chemists have refined the basic formula so that different setting times are available as well as consistency. Accelerators and debonders are available; but once this adhesive gets onto your clothes, I'm afraid that's it!

As an adhesive super-glue has great tensile strength (i.e. it is difficult to pull apart), but very poor shear strength (i.e. you can twist or slide the items apart). It is great for gluing fine detail and gap-filling, plus strengthening joints in plasticard. The problem with super-glue is the potential waste: until recently I estimated that I wasted 95%. I used to apply a drop to a spare piece of plastic and dip with a pin from this drop until I needed another. Depending upon the atmospheric conditions this could be in anything from a few moments to half an hour. By chance I found that if the glue is applied to a spare piece of waxed paper - as found, for example, on double-sided Selotape - then it does not cure. A single drop is sometimes sufficient for a whole evening's modelling.

Children's white glue

This non-toxic glue is especially useful for jobs where no strength is needed, like attaching equipment to the tank or making baggage and flags. It dries to a transparent finish and shrinks while curing. One great advantage of this glue is its ability to reconstitute itself again when wet. The brand I use is American and called *Elmer's Glue-All*.

Abrasive papers

An essential ingredient in modelling is abrasive paper, known in Britain as either sandpaper or wetordry. I use *wetordry* because it lasts longer and is easier to use. All abrasive papers clog quickly with detritus from the material being sanded; but if wetordry is used with water then the excess can simply be washed away. (With conventional sandpaper the use of water would destroy the glue.) The wetordry comes in a variety of grades; I use three, the roughest being P320, a medium grade P600 and the finest P1200. With these three I can achieve any desired finish. In addition to these sheets I also use strips of abrasive paper for miscellaneous sanding.

Epoxy fillers

An indispensable aid to the modeller, these fillers generally come as a two-part application. As with epoxy glue, a chemical reaction takes place when the two agents are mixed. The type I use is universally known as *Milliput*; this cures in approximately three to four hours at room temperature, but can be accelerated by heat. Totally pliable when first mixed, the putty can be used for filling gaps and for moulding difficult shapes. Once dry it becomes rock hard, and can be sawn, filed, sanded or worked in any other normal way. One of the modeller's greatest allies.

General consumables:

Steel wool is also a superb mild abrasive. I use a 0000 gauge wool; normally used on furniture for French polishing, it is perfect for final cleaning of plastic, brass, etc. You will probably not find this gauge in normal hardware shops, and it is best obtained in furniture restorer's shops. You will also use substantial quantities of *Selotape, Blue-tac,* tissues etc.

These, then, are the main tools and materials needed for standard work. The next section covers the more specialist tools needed for conversions, scratch-builds and super-detailing.

SPECIALIST TOOLS

To progress to conversions and scratch-builds, most of the tools detailed below are, if not essential, then certainly a distinct advantage.

P-cutter & Compass cutter

Two highly useful tools for scribing and cutting plasticard. Both cut a V-shape in the plastic and enable the modeller to snap the card for a clean break. Obviously, the compass cutter is designed to cut circular pieces of plastic; diameters from about 10mm to 150mm can be cut.

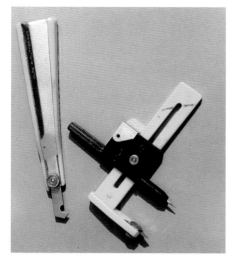

The P-cutter and compass cutter, both indispensable tools for cutting plastic. I made some slight refinements to the compass cutter to enable it to cut smaller diameters than intended.

Punch & die set, round & hexagonal

These two sets, which are available from *Historex Agents* of Dover, are admittedly expensive; but they are well worth the initial cost, and if treated with care will give the modeller a lifetime of use. With a range of hole sizes from about 0.5mm to 4mm, the punch is able to produce an infinite number of bolt heads from plasticard, in thicknesses of from 0.5mm to 1.25mm. The other, hexagonal punch produces nuts. Some vehicles, for example the 38(t) series, have literally hundreds of visible bolts. Costs for the round punch are about £28.00 and for the hexagonal about £35.00 (1995 prices).

Beading tool sets (grainers)

Very similar to the punch and die set but suitable for punching very small diameter holes (from 0.3mm to 1.25mm) in thin aluminium or brass sheet, these are ideal for forming flush rivets in engine decks. You will pay approximately £20.00 for a set of 20 tools. You will also need a piece of vulcanised rubber to tap the rivets out; your ideal source for this would be a worn-out vulcanised rubber mould begged from a friend who casts in white metal.

True Sander

This purpose-made tool is designed to sand plastic or resin to true straight or parallel lines. The discipline of sanding to required lines or angles is one of the most difficult to acquire. This tool, purchased from *Micro Mark* of the USA for approximately £15.00, helps mitigate the problem.

The Chopper

Available from the same company as the True Sander, this tool has a number of cutting functions. By the use of an industrial razor clean, feather-free cuts of plastic strip can be made. Mitred cuts can also be made, and 30, 45 and 60 degree guides are included. An adjustable stop permits duplication of pieces up to 80mm. The cost is around £9.00.

Pyrogravure

This tool is really a sophisticated hot needle powered by a standard electrical source; a transformer steps down the current so that the heat is able to melt little more than plastic. Originally developed for detailing plastic figures, its use in AFV modelling is threefold: delicate battle damage can be recreated; a Zimmerit effect can be applied to light and medium tanks; and it can be used as a soldering iron for low melt solders.

Propane torch

Although this heat source can be used for soldering, the intense heat will equally melt most of the metals you may use in AFV modelling. However, it is sometimes very useful to be able to soften certain metals. Brass, for example, is fairly hard and will not always bend easily. If it is heated until it glows red, then quenched in water, you will find that the metal has lost its rigidity.

Glass-fibre cleaning pens

These lethal little pens are invaluable for cleaning those impossible-to-get-to places. The downside is that while the pen contains a dense, seemingly solid rod of glass-fibre, this is in fact composed of thousands of tiny stems which break very easily. Despite this apparent fragility they are very abrasive and perfect for cleaning. Under no circumstances use them in a dry condition: as the rods snap they are fired into the air, or into you! Being so small

Punch and die sets from Historex Agents - essential for the super-detailer, converter and scratch-builder.

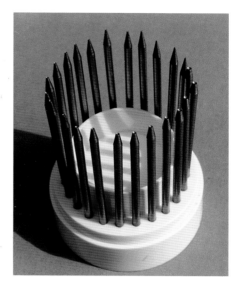

Beading tool set, extraordinarily good value for money; remember you will need printer's aluminium sheet and a small piece of vulcanised rubber to get the most out of this, enabling the mass production of domed bolt/rivet heads.

they present a serious danger and are very difficult to remove once you are impaled. The answer is simple - use them wet, with a solution of dish-washing liquid and water. Should they snap, the rods become immersed in the liquid solution.

Safety

I am sure that most readers will be tempted to skip this section, on a subject which the modeller prefers to forget or believes does not concern him. That the reader has spent a fairly substantial sum on buying this book argues that he is not a casual modeller but an enthusiast, perhaps a veteran of some years' modelling. So it is worth remarking that some of the potential hazards relate to long term exposure - *the use of certain materials over a long period can represent a serious danger to health.* I am not a safety officer; I can only reiterate the warnings found on the packaging of most products, and trust to the readers' common sense.

Many of the tools the modeller uses have a lethal ability to slice or pierce; from time to time we all end up with cuts. Remember that the hobby does generate a lot of detritus - getting lead filings from white metal into an open wound is not going to improve your health. As a minimum precaution keep all wounds clean and covered. (Super-glue works surprisingly well on small cuts and does not hurt when applied!)

We are frequently advised to use some product in a well ventilated room; but most modellers are more prolific in the winter months, when the rest of the family may well object to open doors and windows. There is no single answer to this problem, but every modeller should take it seriously. The fumes from the solvents found in many glues can be genuinely dangerous over the long term. If you cannot ventilate the room then at least be constantly aware of what you are doing, and limit your exposure; keep the lid on the bottle

Right
Right
The Chopper from Micro Mark makes repetitive cutting of plastic strip easy.

Centre
Glass fibre cleaning pens. Ideal tools for cleaning in those impossible nooks and crannies, these should only ever be used with a wetting solution - under no circumstances use them dry. The fine fibres break easily and fly up; if they should get into your eye you will need hospital treatment.

when not in use, and make sure that it cannot tip over - purpose-made or adapted containers are generally safer than the supplied bottle.

The ideal solution to the problem is to use hazardous liquids within the confines of a spray booth, but few of us are able to purchase this equipment. The principle of this apparatus is that the air and fumes are expelled by means of a fan through a filter and then via a hose to the outside air. If you are a kit-basher then you may well be using your airbrush a great deal, and this equipment is certainly worth considering as a long term investment. You may also consider making one yourself. It is not very difficult: you only need an extractor fan, a booth, and tumble-dryer hose - but remember that it needs to be flameproofed, as most of the solvents used are highly volatile. (This is also a point well worth bearing in mind by modellers who are habitual smokers; an open bottle of solvent and a Zippo are a potentially deadly combination.)

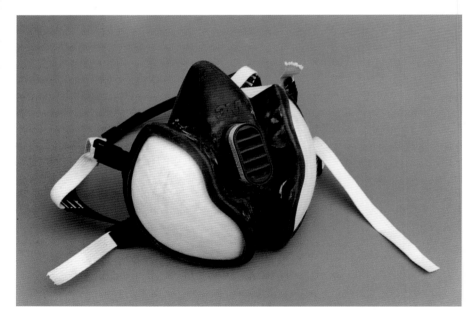

The other solution to fumes is to wear a mask. The best are termed *organic vapour/ particulate respirators*, and can be bought at any reasonable hardware shop. For about £15 - the cost of a modest kit - you can enjoy full protection; if you can get one which takes replacement filters, so much the better. A simple test to check when they need replacing is whether you can smell the solvents, etc.; the air you breathe through the filters should be free of any smell - if it isn't, change filters.

Most modellers will at some time also use or work on polyurethane resin. In its solid state the resin can be worked like any other hard inert material - it can be sawn, filed and polished. But you should avoid using powered tools to cut, file or sand the resin: fine silica dust is then thrown into the air and, if you are not using a mask, inhaled into your lungs. The long term effect of this is not fully understood, but it is certainly harmful. Use hand saws or files to cut and shape; if you need to sand the resin then use wetordry paper with the resin dipped into water. Keep the resin wet; not only will this be safe, but it will give a better finish and also preserves the paper.

Although not directly related to personal hazards, the wearing of a modelling apron will ensure that your wife/girlfriend also remains non-hazardous. I have ruined many shirts and pairs of trousers by careless use of super-glue, paint, and solvents. I am too lazy to change when I get home from work, so the apron has proved its worth many times.

Most aspects of safety are common sense; if you want to be still around and modelling when you are old, then adopt safe working practices and stick to them.

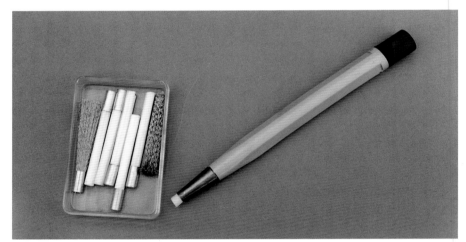

Above
An organic vapour/particulate respirator, the minimum safety requirement when airbrushing with solvents.

CHAPTER TWO
REFERENCE MATERIAL

f I were to be asked the one single reason for any success that I may have achieved in modelling German AFVs, I would answer "reference". Since starting in the hobby I have become a voracious collector of all reference material on German fighting vehicles of the period 1933-45. I have accumulated hundreds of books and plans and literally thousands of photographs, both contemporary action pictures and modern museum studies. The collection and collation of this material has almost become a hobby in itself; and a home computer to file and retrieve this information is certainly an advantage. Once a project is decided upon the collection of information should begin. This may take days or months, depending upon the level of detail sought. (What is certain is that the one piece of information that you did not manage to obtain will automatically turn up a few days after the project is complete - this mysterious phenomenon appears to be familiar to most keen modellers...)

Despite a renaissance in German AFV modelling over the last five years, much conflicting information is still circulating. Most of the problems relate to the identification of a vehicle as a particular type, mark, or model (Ausführung). There was no black and white rule as to exactly when alterations caused a vehicle to change its Ausführung designation. Obviously, factories manufacturing vehicles did not introduce modifications overnight; this would have caused serious disruption to production lines.

Below
Further afield - but if you do have the opportunity to visit the United States, then the Aberdeen Proving Ground's rusting but wide-ranging open air collection of vehicles is well worth the trip for the invaluable opportunity to study and photograph the real thing close up.

There would have been a grey area, with vehicles receiving the modifications progressively. Add to this the complication of damaged vehicles returned to the factories for repair and refit, and you have sufficient reason for many of the dilemmas that plague the modeller. It is commonplace to find what may appear to be contradictory evidence in photographs. My only advice is to study carefully all the plans, drawings and photographs you can lay hands on, and to read any relevant books. There is too great a tendency to rely exclusively on pictorial evidence; answers may sometimes be found as readily in text as in photographs.

How does the modeller obtain this reference material? Books are the cheapest and most accessible means of information, and later in this chapter I describe those publications which will give the modeller a comprehensive grounding in the subject. Many recent books are directly orientated towards the modeller, with most plans in 1:35 scale, and historical information on units, theatres of operations, etc.

My photographic collection of museum vehicles now runs to nearly 12,000 images of over 200 pieces of equipment; they range from 200-plus photographs of some vehicles to a single shot of others. These photographs

Above
The French Army tank museum at Saumur contains one of the world's best preserved and restored collections; here the author (second from left) and friends are on a visit to photograph German vehicles. These days it is no longer a hugely expensive or complicated undertaking to travel to the major European museums, which offer a wealth of research possibilities.

are very much my pride and joy, and are my constant companions while I am modelling. I took many of them while visiting museums in Britain, France, Germany and the USA; the rest I have traded with modellers from around the world. Requests for information in military modelling magazines and through such specialist associations as MAFVA (Miniature Armoured Fighting Vehicles Association) invariably find a sympathetic response from like-minded enthusiasts. Most of my friendships have developed from initial responses to such requests. The currency of such exchanges varies according to the respective needs of the writers - photographs, models, and tools all provide the necessary ingredients for mutual satisfaction.

Visits to museums are of course an ideal way of obtaining your own photographic

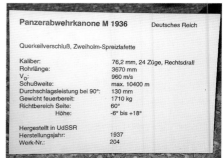

Panzerabwehrkanone M 1936	Deutsches Reich
Querkeilverschluß, Zweiholm-Spreizlafette	

Kaliber:	76,2 mm, 24 Züge, Rechtsdrall
Rohrlänge:	3670 mm
V_0:	960 m/s
Schußweite:	max. 10400 m
Durchschlagsleistung bei 90°:	130 mm
Gewicht feuerbereit:	1710 kg
Richtbereich Seite:	60°
Höhe:	-6° bis +18°
Hergestellt in UdSSR	
Herstellungsjahr:	1937
Werk-Nr.:	204

Left
The degree of fine detail which can be studied, recorded with photographs, and personally measured during such museum visits is invaluable when later trying to understand plans and drawings and when super-detailing models.

Above
Remember to photograph the vehicle's data boards at the same time - these are essential for the proper cataloguing of your photograph collection.

reference. Most museums will allow photography for personal use, with some attaching conditions for commercial reasons (a museum's existence depends on visitors, and therefore it is only reasonable that some conditions are imposed). Most curators are very willing to assist modellers in their projects. A stamped addressed envelope should be the minimum you send with any request, and a small donation, e.g. to cover photocopying costs, will be greatly appreciated. You must also consider that the curator and his team are there primarily to preserve historical vehicles, not to answer the infinite number of questions that modellers can ask. Be reasonable and specific in your requests for information. If you try to master the technical descriptions of vehicle parts, this will help the professional team in answering your questions.

Many vehicles in museum collections have been restored by teams of enthusiastic amateurs. These renovations should be treated with a degree of caution; regrettably, even some quite recent refurbishments have born little relationship to historical reality. Hopefully, in the next few years the German AFV modeller will be treated to the release of substantial amounts of information from museums beyond the former Iron Curtain.

With the exception of the *Victory Museum* in Belgium and the *Kubinka Museum* in Russia, I have written to all the main museums that house substantial collections of German vehicles, requesting details of their collection, opening times, and any photographic restrictions. I was interested not only in obtaining this information, but also in checking the response time. *The Tank Museum, Bovington* came out top with a reply in only five days, while *Saumur* was last, at 63 days (see Appendix for the addresses and response times). All answered my queries, and the *Panzer Museum, Munster* even included a substantial publication on their

collection. Both of the military museums in the USA which I visited in the spring of 1995 were overwhelmingly helpful and hospitable. It is a great experience just to see the "real life" subject of your models; but it is also valuable opportunity to collect your own reference material. A competent modeller should learn how to accurately measure, sketch, and photograph the subject.

For readers who do not have the opportunity to visit museums, books are the obvious alternative source of information. Any serious modeller will have a steadily increasing library - my own now exceeds 400 titles, ranging from booklets of a few pages to definitive tomes on single vehicles. It is not possible to list here even a proportion of the titles that I possess; so my comments below are limited to those publications which I consider the essential basis for the serious German AFV modeller.

The Japanese have always had an enormous

interest in German World War II forces and equipment; with their natural inclination to precision and thoroughness, they have produced some outstanding publications catering specifically for the modeller. From the printed accreditations the sources of the photographs are invariably the same as we can find; but their attention to detail and standard of publication frequently make their books uniquely helpful to the modeller.

Readers must understand that any comments here recommending a certain publication, model or other product are purely my personal opinions - others may well have different views. Further details of publications mentioned here will be found in the Appendix.

The most outstanding publications to date are those produced by Dai Nippon Kaiga / Art Box under the titles *Achtung Panzer* and *Panzers in Saumur* - a number of different books have been published under each title.

Right
My photographs are my constant companions during construction of a model.

The *Achtung* series have concentrated to date on the Panzerkampfwagen III, IV and V series. The information contained in these books, whilst mostly of a sketch type, does include plans and photographs (mostly unpublished elsewhere). Infinite detail is illustrated, down to differences that may only concern a single bolt. The text is mostly in Japanese, but the captions are bilingual. These books are really a compendium of information published in their monthly modelling magazine *Model Graphics*; and to judge from the material which has appeared in this journal, there are many books still to be released . *Panzers in Saumur* selects vehicles from the collection of that museum for very thorough in-depth reviews, including scale drawings, detailed sketches and a wealth of photographs. These books are generally priced in the £15-£25 range.

One of the essential reference works is the *Encyclopaedia of German Tanks of World War II*. This is a complete illustrated directory of German battle tanks, armoured cars, self-propelled guns and semi-tracked vehicles of 1933-45. Although brief in its description of each vehicle, it includes the technical essentials, measurements, history, specific features and combat service.

With regard to camouflage and divisional and tactical markings I would recommend the three volumes of *Panzer Colours* by Bruce Culver. These will give the serious modeller an in-depth review of this very extensive subject. For the purist who requires the definitive publication on tactical markings I would suggest *Leo Niehorster's German World War II Organisational Series* as the definitive works on this vast subject. (Six volumes have already been published, and the series is only up to June 1941 so far...).

After only one or two years' modelling I came across the *Speilberger German Armour & Military Vehicles Series*. There are a total of 15 volumes in the series, and other than No.1 all are devoted to World War Two vehicles. These are justifiably considered to be the definitive works on German vehicles of the period. The drawback is that they are in German; but increasingly, individual volumes are being reprinted in English. When first published they were not orientated towards the modeller's needs, but fortunately the author/publisher is nowadays gearing much of the information towards this readership.

Right
A wartime photo of a late model Brummbär provides perfect reference to the exact appearance of its Zimmerit coating.

Prices vary in the range between £20 and £35.

While these are the books which I consider indispensable, there are, of course, many other publications well worth considering. For example, Uwe Feist's and Bruce Culver's new Ryton Publications on the *Tiger 1*, *Tiger and SturmTiger* and *Panther* are outstanding works which we may hope will be the first of a new generation of books specifically catering for the modeller and historian combined. If, like me, you have a continuing love affair with the Tiger, then the new Fedorowicz publication by Wolfgang Schneider, *Tiger in Combat*, is the finest book to date on this subject. The history of every unit issued with this vehicle is treated in a depth never achieved before; this information, and the hundreds of previously unpublished photographs, are testimony to the author's astonishing success in contacting surviving Tiger veterans. The history, camouflage and many other unique details of every unit's Tigers make this inevitably expensive book good value.

It is wise to cross-reference all your reference material; even illustrious publications like those mentioned above sometimes include conflicting information. At the end of the day you may need to make a rational choice between sources based upon the information you have available. (Be prepared to justify this to your colleagues or judges at any show for you may enter the resulting model...).

Right
The easiest source of reference material: all serious modellers will accumulate books - my own collection now runs to many hundreds. Given the prices we pay nowadays for high quality kits, etched sets, specialist accessories and tools, to risk spoiling weeks of work for lack of the accurate information or relevant photograph in a book costing a few more pounds is a false economy.

CHAPTER THREE
MODELS AVAILABLE

Since I started modelling I have experienced using the products of many manufacturers; and I include here those series which I believe are important to the German AFV modeller. Most are included because of their quality, a few because of the size of their range. I would recommend the reader to the Japanese publication by Dai Nippon Kaiga, *Panzer File 94/95*. Published annually since 1992, this lists the products of all manufacturers who produce material in this field. Lavishly illustrated with examples of the products, this is an essential source for the serious modeller. A word of caution concerning the illustrations: these are more an indication of the modeller's ability than the quality of the product displayed. In this chapter of the present book, my references to manufacturers are based on the overall quality of their ranges rather than upon an indiviudal product.

Major manufacturers

In the field of mass-production injection-moulded plastic kits there are only three main contenders. Two, Tamiya and Italeri, have been pillars of the hobby for many years, and have recently started to produce new German subjects after an absence of about a decade; the third, Dragon, is a new contender. *Tamiya*, who have the largest product range (although much of it is rather old), have in my opinion achieved the premier position within the industry with the release of their latest kits. Modellers once used to paying about £10.00 for their Tamiya kits will now find that this has at least doubled and in some cases trebled. The old models from *Italeri* were in my opinion the best on the market and, in comparable cases, far superior to other manufacturers. These old models are still outstanding, and cheap at around £10 per kit. However, I believe that these roles have now been reversed: Italeri's new kits are not of a comparable quality to Tamiya's, but they represent the best value for money.

The newcomer *Dragon* has a prolific output of kits, with a breath-taking new release apparently almost monthly. My initial reaction to the first Dragon kits was one of disappointment; standards of accuracy and attention to detail seemed to me more akin to those of the mid-1970s. If these kits were very cheap then there might be some mitigation, but this is not the case, and in Britain they retail for £20.00 - £35.00. There seemed to be some commercial agreement between Dragon and Italeri in spring 1995, as Dragon kits appeared to be reaching the market under the Italeri name and at Italeri prices. The StuG III Ausf B is the first Dragon kit that I feel able genuinely to praise for a high degree of accuracy; attention to some small detail is still disappointing, but Dragon are certainly getting there. Since the StuG's introduction all subsequent Dragon kits are of a much

Top

An example of a contemporary injection moulded plastic kit from Tamiya, offering very high quality and a good standard of accuracy. Tamiya supply a plastic kit with the option of purchasing additional refinements. Dragon Models generally include an etched set, individual track links, etc.

Above

Gunze Sangyo's "high tech" Panzerkampfwagen IV, priced at over £120. At these prices it makes sense for an experienced and well equipped modeller to weigh up the comparative cost and difficulty of converting and super-detailing a less expensive basic kit using personally assembled extras.

improved quality and to be highly recommended.

The only other substantial contender in the injection moulded market, though small by comparison, is *Nichimo*. Their product range is limited to the five heavy tanks that were released more than a decade ago, of reasonable quality for that time but at a disadvantage when compared to current products. Both *Hasegawa* and *ESCI* have isolated German vehicles in their range.

"High tech" kits

Perhaps the most unusual of all the kit manufacturers is *Gunze Sangyo*, who describe their kits as "high tech". I believe this to be, in general, a much abused phase; and while I would certainly describe their products as high quality, I do not personally consider the kits to be at the very frontier of quality and accuracy. It is not possible to generalise about the materials used in these kits. Some are "100% Gunze", with plastic, white and etched metal components; others use another manufacturer's basic kit with various improvements. The field and anti-tank gun kits are entirely of white metal. Comparison of the average quality and the prices (rarely under £60.00, and in some cases, e.g. the PzKfw IV Ausf G, well over £100.00) leads me to doubt that they represent particularly good value for money. The plastic parts, if produced by Gunze, are excellent in quality. The white metal castings are of very good quality but frequently contain details - e.g. tool clasps - which are cast on; the removal of detail on white metal is not easy.

One interesting question is how much effort, and extra expense, the modeller should have to go to in order to super-detail a "high tech" kit. The etched set usually given with the kit is of good quality, but not up to the standard of the products of mid-1990s contemporaries like The Show Modelling.

Smaller specialist manufacturers

Apart from these main manufacturers there is a very substantial "cottage industry" of small, specialist kit producers. The material mostly employed is resin, supplemented frequently by

white metal, which is far more robust for the production of detailed parts. There are in excess of 30 manufacturers around the world producing either complete vehicle kits, conversion parts or accessories. In this chapter I mention only those of whose products I have had personal experience, and who produce complete kits and not just conversions or accessories (these latter will be found in Chapter Four).

Most modellers will be familiar with resin kits. Resin is a two-part liquid composed of the resin and a hardener. Most AFV resins are polyurethane, which can be treated like any other hard material when modelling. The resin is cast into RTV (room temperature vulcanised) rubber moulds, generally single but sometimes two-piece. The term "user-friendly" is employed here to describe manufacturers' resin products. Most professionals use a small spacer block between the kit part and the main pouring block. If this method is not employed then the modeller has a time-consuming and frequently difficult job to remove this surplus resin.

The technique of resin casting is labour-intensive and does not lend itself to mass production; accordingly all kits are hand made, with prices to match, generally in the £40.00 - £70.00 range.

Perhaps the most professional of these small companies is *Accurate Armour* from Scotland. Regrettably their German subject range is fairly small, as they concentrate mainly on contemporary vehicles; but the presentation of the product is as high as that of the best of the industrial-scale manufacturers. A combination of user-friendly resin, white metal and etched sets normally make up their kits, and their high degree of accuracy makes these a pleasure to build.

Armour Accessories to date have a single complete German vehicle in their range, the almost "science fiction" Minenräumer; this is a resin, white metal and etched brass kit. As I was responsible for the master I cannot give a truly unbiased opinion, but to date all reviews have been very favourable. This is the first in a series of the more unusual vehicles that actually saw service.

The most prolific manufacturer is the French company *Azimuth/ADV*, with a substantial selection of products the greater proportion of which are German. The quality of the resin is quite superb, arguably the best on the market. Depending on where *Azimut/ADV* obtain their white metal castings, which vary from kit to kit, the modeller will find a diversity of quality from outstanding to mediocre. Etched sets are frequently incorporated within the kits. The subsidiary product name of *Ironside* denotes kits with a multitude of different materials including injection moulded plastic. Very user-friendly resin casting techniques make these kits a joy to build; if the product does have a weakness it is the brevity of the instructions, which can lead to unnecessary work and frustration. High degree of scale accuracy.

Cromwell Models of Scotland have a large and excellent product range with, until recently, a strong emphasis on the Panther series. With the recent re-entry of the major manufacturers into the market their range has been somewhat duplicated. It is probable that the Panther series may be discontinued. However, Cromwell still have a varied and very interesting range, from the small light Panzers to the "drawing board" vehicles of the future. Very user-friendly, and unusual in that the kits are 100% resin with all fine detail frequently cast on. Exceptionally skilled casting techniques ensure that this detail is reproduced, but it can be very fragile and requires careful handling. High degree of scale accuracy.

Mini Art Studios of Hong Kong market an unusual and expanding product range of exclusively resin kits of equipment conversions and complete vehicles. When their first models of small German field guns came onto the market they were generally hailed as the best resin productions in the world. Good quality resin with user-friendly manufacturing procedures make these a pleasure to construct.

Scale Model Accessories have an expanding range of softskin vehicles and support equipment; their kits are of a similar composition to Azimut/ADV with a resin/white metal mix. The resin is generally user-friendly and of an acceptable quality; this is not always true of the white metal components.

Sovereign Models specialise in Blitzkrieg era vehicles, with a range of Spahwagens and Pzkfw III/StuGs. Kits are composed of very user-friendly resin, as good as any on the market, with small detail cast in white metal. Sovereign also have a white metal figure range. The expertise gained in figure production has been used to good effect to cast everything from fine detail to complex tracks. Probably the cheapest range on the market, at £30.00 - £50.00.

H&K35(NKC) from Belgium have a small product range, which currently tends to revolve around the s.WS vehicle. They must be considered a high quality resin producer, even though the press mould technique used for all parts other than main components is not very user-friendly, leaving a thin mould line which though easy to clean is sometimes tedious. Good accuracy and attractive vehicles.

Precision Models, also from Belgium, have a limited range of field and anti-tank gun models exclusively of resin. Very accurate and finely detailed kits, but distinctly unfriendly in use: the lack of spacer blocks means that the

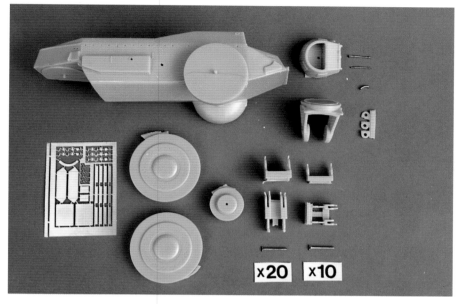

Above
What the modeller may expect to get from a high quality "cottage industry" manufacturer: a kit incorporating components in resin, white metal and etched brass - in this case Armour Accessories' Minenräumer (see Chapter Nine for photos of the completed model).

Left
The converter's and scratch-builder's best friend in time of need - the spares box. A wide range of "left-overs" can accumulate surprisingly quickly; if you thoughtlessly discard anything, you can bet on needing it later.

modeller has to remove a substantial block of resin from every item, with consequent risk of damage to the detail. However, for accuracy and detail they have no competitors; and there are plans to expand the German artillery range.

AL.BY. are a French company with a limited range of German vehicles. User-friendly casting techniques, together with accuracy and quality make these well worth considering. Also has a single injection moulded plastic kit, the Panhard armoured car, which is very good quality.

DES, another French company, has a varied range with a limited number of German vehicles including some of the larger prime movers. User-friendly techniques with a good degree of accuracy.

Verlinden is almost certainly the largest of the independent specialists, with a capacity approaching even the injection moulding giants. Very few full German resin kits, the majority of their production being geared to conversions and accessories. High quality definition sometimes spoilt by inaccuracies, both in detail and scale; a huge product range, very popular with most modellers.

Two German companies, *Hecker & Goros* and *Puchala*, produce white metal field, anti-tank and anti-aircraft guns. Regrettably these tend to be in 1:32 scale; when used in isolation this may not be of great importance, but when incorporated in a conversion it may cause problems. Hecker & Goros use a sandblast finish to the white metal which gives

a beautifully clean appearance. Both very high quality and worth considering.

With the exception of Precision, Sovereign and H&K35(NKC), all the above companies also produce substantial figure and accessories ranges.

*　　*　　*

Many purchases by modellers are made via mail order, with the attendant risk that the product and quality may not be exactly what you had anticipated. There is therefore an onus on modellers who review kits to give the reader a fair and unbiased opinion. Regrettably, some magazine kit review sections are little more than free advertising sections for manufacturers. Other magazines give a true opinion; but the number of kits reviewed compared to the number of releases is inevitably tiny. It would be refreshing if all reviewers remembered that their first duty is to the modeller, and not to either the kit manufacturers or the advertising manager of the magazine.

If you purchase an item by mail order within your own country then its return if unsatisfactory is straightforward, with various legal safeguards. If you purchase unsatisfactory products from abroad, then returning them and obtaining a refund can present serious problems. If possible find out whether there is a distributor in your country; and ask friends or local modelling groups about a particular company before making what can be a substantial outlay.

CHAPTER FOUR
CONSTRUCTION & SUPER-DETAILING

Before beginning this chapter on constructing kits it is important to make the point that all the comments made and techniques described represent my personal standard. To the vast majority of readers this is only a hobby; enjoyment and personal satisfaction from your efforts should be the overriding consideration. It is not important to follow all the styles and techniques described in this book. This is how I model; if by selecting some or all of the techniques you improve your models and your satisfaction, then we will both have achieved something. Other than the interpretation of camouflage, everything is a matter of patient practice and technique.

PLASTIC KITS

Most serious modellers find their way into the hobby through a period of "kit-bashing". Many of the basic modelling skills will be acquired in this period. When I first started modelling I was producing a new model about every two weeks. While my construction techniques have improved considerably since

those days, my painting ability has at best remained static, if not actually declined. I now make only about six to eight models a year - not enough to keep my hand in with the airbrush.

To produce a model straight from the box requires very few tools; a hobby knife, side-cutting pliers, wetdry abrasive paper, and plastic glue are the only essentials. A power drill will also help improve the deficiencies in some kits. It seems unnecessary to say it, but do spend an hour or two reading and understanding the sequence of the plans, and if necessary programme the painting into the construction phase (this will normally only apply to open-topped vehicles or the interiors of soft-skin cabs, etc.).

Once you understand the sequence and instructions, then remove the plastic parts from the sprue in the recommended order. The sprue is the superfluous "tree" of plastic to which the parts of the kit are attached. This sprue is formed from the injection of liquid plastic into a two-piece steel mould at very high temperatures. The liquid plastic solidifies in the mould and, once cooled, the sprue

supporting the kit parts is removed. The process of forming the detail within the steel mould is extremely expensive and therefore the manufacturer needs a substantial run to recover his costs. When the mould is new and well made the part should be virtually free of seam lines. However, over a period of time the steel moulds deteriorate and plastic seeps into the adjacent areas, creating "flash". The two halves of the mould can also slip out of alignment, producing, for instance, pieces with an elliptical rather than a round section. In "kit-bashing" the main chore is removing the flash and producing a seamless part.

Below
An example of super-detailing; even with a kit as good as Dragon's StuG Ausf F, some additional fine detailing is always necessary - the technical limitations of injection moulding make some undercuts and other small details impossible to reproduce. This model was completed using a specialised etched set, white metal spares, cotton cables, lead and aluminium foil clasps, etc.

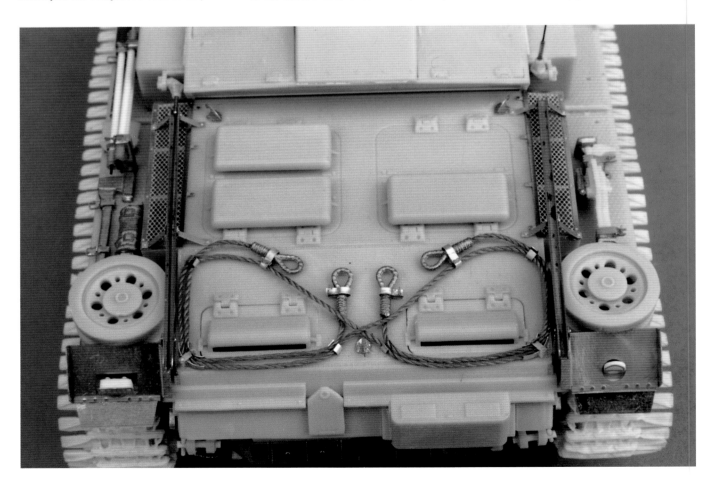

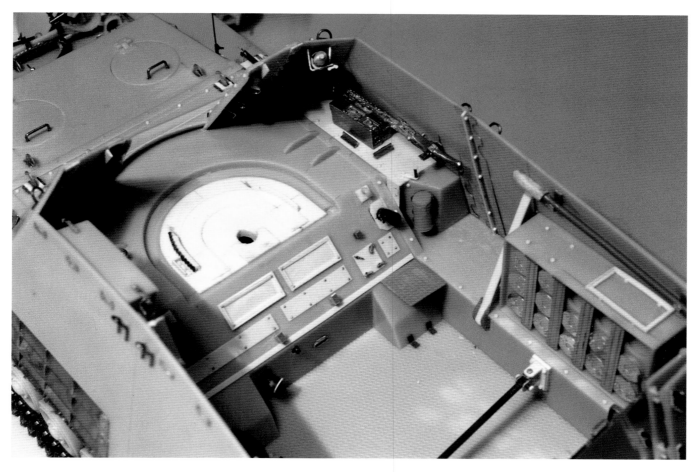

First we need to remove the part from the sprue; do not bend the item off the sprue, use the side-cutters to detach it. Tamiya and Italeri kits should present no problems; but I have occasionally experienced some difficulty with Dragon kits. It is not unknown for the surplus injection sprue to break off into the kit part leaving a section of plastic to replace. If this should be the case, use a circular saw in your drill at a slow speed. Once free of the sprue the mould line can be cleaned up with either knife or wetordry paper. Right-handed people should hold the part in the left hand and draw the knife blade back towards the body. Once the seam has nearly disappeared use the wetordry, grade P600, to bring the surface to a good finish. One of the main painting techniques you will need to master is dry-brushing. This most simple of painting methods has one major drawback: it is totally unsympathetic to poorly finished surfaces, and will throw into stark relief any mould lines, glue residues, etc. Metallic finishes are the most unforgiving, so particular attention should be paid to obtaining the very smoothest surface on these items. I sometimes use the silicon rubber discs in my motor drill; they can be extremely delicate in their abrasive qualities.

Gluing and filling

Once the plastic parts are cleaned up, check the fit; and with an old No.00 sable brush apply glue to the joint. Powerful solvents will flow along the joint by capillary action, so you will not need to brush glue along the whole junction. Try to avoid thick glues,

which make it hard to keep a clean joint. Keep your fingers out of the way - perfect finger prints can easily be etched into the surface of the plastic by capillary action, and are very difficult to remove. (If it should occur, wait a few minutes until the plastic is dry and then apply super-glue to the damaged area; again allow to dry; then use wetordry to restore the surface. If the damage is very severe, apply baking powder to the super-glue; you will then have a rock hard surface to rework to shape.)

Good kits should not have gaps between joints. Sometimes through mistakes on your part this occurs, and there are always the occasional badly fitting kits. If the gap is very small then use super-glue. I use a thin piece of wire in a pin-vice; apply the glue to the waxed surface of double-sided Selotape and draw from this reservoir. Use instant super-glue as this is the thinnest and flows the best. If the gap-filling exercise is in an accessible place where it can be sanded after drying, then large gaps can be filled with the additional of baking power; apply super-glue and baking powder in repetitive stages until the joint is overfilled. There is no need to wait, the joint will be hard at once and can be filed or sanded.

In more inaccessible positions I would recommend the use of Milliput two-part epoxy putty. Once fully cured (three/four hours at room temperature) this can be filed, sawn or polished. One distinct advantage is that if placed in contact with water during the curing stage it develops great adhesive qualities, and can also be brought to a very smooth finish. Large gaps can be filled, using

Above

The author chose to super-detail Dragon's Hummel kit to such an extent that the result almost bordered on conversion/ scratch-building, employing plastic, white metal, an etched set, and a completely new gun.

a spatula or wax carver to achieve a reasonably smooth surface. Next take a good quality flat red sable, and with copious quantities of water "paint" the joint until all surplus Milliput is removed. Once it is dry no further action should be required.

Tracks

In the mid-1990s kits come with either soft vinyl one-piece tracks or individual track links. Some years ago Model Kasten produced their first individual track links for the Panther; since then most kit manufacturers have introduced these either as standard parts of the kit (Dragon), or still use vinyl (Tamiya & Italeri) with the option of buying the individual links as an accessory. The quality of the vinyl tracks has come a long way since the crudity of the 1970s and early 1980s; they are really quite acceptable provided they are installed correctly. To ensure that tracks hang correctly it is important to study photographs. Real tank tracks are very heavy castings, and because they are flexibly linked they sag between any two supported parts (this sag is correctly described as the catenary action). On some tanks the appearance of this sag was quite distinct; the Panther is perhaps the prime

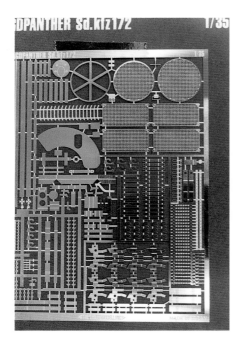

Above

The Show Modelling's Jagdpanther set. The degree of detail offered by these etched brass sets certainly tests the modeller's ability to work with minute, ultra-fine components.This company's products are probably the best of their type in the world, and are consequently expensive.

example, with the tracks hanging in a beautiful curve from the drive sprocket almost to the sixth wheel station back. Obviously a new tank with freshly tensioned tracks shows very little sag, but after a short time in the field this effect becomes more apparent. The recreation of this effect using individual links is very easy, but with one-piece vinyl tracks it is a little more time-consuming.

If you are modelling tracks using individual links it is best if all wheels, including the drive sprocket and rear idler, are installed first. If you have the facility to make them "revolvable", then keep it - on occasion it is a distinct advantage. Later they can be glued into their permanent position. To keep the tracks in position during assembly I make a small jig from two pieces of plastic strip, 3mm x 5mm, and attach it to my working surface by double-sided tape. Depending on the type of track I adjust their parallel position so that the track tooth sits snugly in the gap.

Once I used to temporarily install the tracks for shape and position; this would be done in two halves, top and bottom, with the joins at the drive sprocket and rear idler. I could never understand why when I later came to install the tracks after painting the two joins would never match; there was always a gap. The answer was that the plastic shrinks. Since I deduced this I have installed the tracks first and painted them later.

Once you have sufficient unglued track on your jig to cover the length from half the drive sprocket to half the rear idler, apply plastic glue liberally and leave to dry for about five minutes. Once the track is fairly rigid, then - starting from the rear idler - feed the track to

the drive sprocket, over any top return rollers. Position the track over the sprocket but do not glue it. Repeat the process with the bottom tracks until you join the two, at sprocket and idler. It may be necessary to gently part all links in the bottom run to get a good fit if the tracks appear too short, or to push the links together if the fit is too slack. Once you are happy with the fit you can adjust the top run of track to recreate the correct sag. With, e.g., a small screw driver, apply gentle downwards pressure at the appropriate points; you may need to repeat this a few times until the plastic dries. Once you are satisfied with the installation, glue the tracks to the wheels to make a permanent attachment.

Vinyl tracks present a few more problems than individual links and are not of a comparable quality or appearance. However, the newer offerings from Tamiya or Italeri are much improved and with careful installation will produce a good appearance. Many years ago, when vinyl tracks were the only option, I made up a little tool to weld the tracks together, from a small flat-headed nail hammered into a piece of wood. The nail is heated, using a lighter, and applied to the pins of the joint. It is better to have a very hot nail head, as a warm surface only reduces the vinyl to a stringy mess. The application of the heated nail needs to be precise and quick; if contact lasts too long, which in practice is probably only two seconds, the nail will burn through the track. The tip of a pyrogravure can be used to seal adjacent vinyl to improve the strength of the joint.

The painting of small diameter road wheels is very tedious, especially if they are already installed on the tank; but with vinyl tracks they can sometimes be positioned after the painting process, making both the painting of the wheels and the fitting of the track easier - manipulating the tracks around drive sprockets, return rollers, road wheels and idlers is not easy. For smaller tanks, i.e. PzKfw IV and under, once the track is installed, place the first and last road wheel to tension the track. I would recommend that the road wheels of all larger vehicles, e.g. Tigers and Panthers, are fully installed before placing the tracks.

To recreate the sag in vinyl tracks requires the fitting of pins to force the tracks down into position. I use dress maker's pins, 0.7mm in diameter and approximately 18mm long, with the heads snipped off. It is best to use a drill bit fractionally smaller in diameter than the pin to give a good fit without gluing; fortunately there is a standard bit which is perfect for this role - 0.6mm diameter, or No.72 (0.025 inch). Push the track down with the bit; once the correct sag is achieved, drill through the plastic hull side wall. Remember that the bottom of the sag is always midway between the supports. Repeat this process along the length of the track. With pliers, place the pin on top of the track and push down until the hole is located, then push the pin through the plastic wall. Further adjustment of sag can be made by bending the pins. Try and ensure that the pin is between two links and not on top of the running surface of the link; once painted black the pin will become invisible.

After thorough washing in a soapy solution and rinsing in water your model, straight from the box, is now ready to paint.

RESIN KITS

These kits need little different handling from the plastic type, apart from the characteristic that the modeller is normally working with a solid component - it is rare to have to join two halves of a part. The main problems with resin kits spring from production techniques. The products of the best manufacturers will present none of these problems, while poorer quality kits could confront you with all of them.

A constant problem with resin kits is the tendency to warp. This is common in thin section parts, but fortunately rare on main components. The solution is normally simple: immersion in very hot water, and reshaping. Before undertaking this remedial action ensure that you are able to restore the shape to its original form. For example, if you have to bend back to a straight line a long thin shape which has warped to a curve, don't think that after immersion you can use your eye and hand to achieve this - your eye and hand will create an undulating series of small, uneven curves.... Immerse it in very hot water, then flatten it on a hard level surface until cool.

Another problem experienced with resin kits is air bubbles. The best manufacturers use a system of de-gassing the resin, a simple solution to a problem that has plagued the industry since the early days. The resin, once mixed and poured into the mould, is placed in a vacuum chamber and the air is removed by a pump; this also removes the air bubbles which are formed during the mixing process. While this system removes most of the air, it is not 100% guaranteed. Should your model contain exposed air bubble cavities then they are best dealt with by the application of super-glue to small holes, and Milliput to larger ones. Once cured the surface should be rubbed down with fine wetordry paper.

Most resin moulds are made in one piece, so the modeller should not experience problems with seam lines. As mentioned, the professional companies incorporate small spacer blocks of resin; these can be removed with any sharp tool, and the surface cleaned up with wetordry paper. Should the mould be two-piece any seam line can be removed in the same manner as from plastic.

Finally there are those manufacturers of resin kits who adopt "user-unfriendly" techniques. This means that the pouring sprue is directly attached to the component. Resin is a very hard, inert material, and extensive sawing, filing or sanding is not an easy task. The modeller may well consider the use of power tools to assist, but this presents a particular health hazard, as described at the end of Chapter One. If you insist on using powered tools then you **must** wear a safety mask. The safest method is regrettably slow, pure hard labour with hand saw or file.

If sanding, use wetordry with ample quantities of water. Accurate sanding is one of the most difficult skills to learn. There is no easy answer, but as a rule, never sand in one direction only. Ensure that you can grip the object firmly, and apply even pressure to all areas. Never sand up and down when reducing thickness - use a circular motion. Count approximately how many motions; turn through 180 degrees and repeat; now turn 90 degrees and repeat; then turn a final 180 degrees. This should ensure a consistent reduction in the material being sanded.

Once the parts are free of warping and seam

lines and fully prepared, then either super-glue or epoxy glue work very well on resin. The separation of resin parts once super-glued together is virtually impossible, requiring cutting, and I would therefore recommend a non-instant brand of super-glue, or epoxy. If a strong joint is required, e.g. one that will support the weight of the model, then opt for the epoxy. I do not normally like to use epoxy because it is messy, but any excess can be removed with a cocktail stick immediately after the epoxy has become cured. If you clean the joints within approximately 30 minutes of gluing then a crisp, neat joint can be achieved.

The main problem of resin AFV assembly concerns track installation, and regrettably I have had failures as well as success. The cleaning up of resin tracks is perhaps the most tedious of all modelling chores; I have no short cuts - you need a new blade in the knife, a set of fine files, and a lot of patience. Use the glass-fibre pen, under water, to complete the process.

The hard part is the installation. The manufacturers of resin kits rarely provide instructions which programme the construction in a sequence; they tend simply to show where the parts go, and leave it to you to work out the sequence. Every vehicle is different; but do not install the mudguards, skirt plates, etc. before the tracks. If you can feed the top track in one complete section then do so. Glue a sufficient section to reach from the drive sprocket to the rear idler. Once the track spans this distance, then I use an eye dropper full of boiling water to apply locally to the tracks I wish to bend. For example, this method on the drive sprocket limits the affected areas. Once the correct position is achieved use super-glue to fix it permanently. Working back from the drive sprocket, position the track over a return roller, allowing for sag, and continue gluing and positioning. The lower half of the track is much easier. It is important to have a reasonable length of track to complete the installation. If it is too short then you can easily immerse it in boiling water and stretch, or constrict it if too long.

Once the model is complete, wash thoroughly in soapy water to remove any release agents from the resin.

WHITE METAL KITS

Most white metal kits are composed of either bismuth with a lead mixture (42% to 58% respectively), or - much less commonly - pewter, which is almost 100% pure tin. The rarity of pewter kits is due not only to its higher price but also to the higher casting temperatures needed and the relative difficulty of working the metal. White metal AFV kits at 1:35 scale are very rare and generally restricted to field or anti-tank guns. Gunze, and to a lesser extent Hecker & Goros and Puchala are the main producers.

As with resin, production is by hand and prices consequently high. From the master or sub-master a vulcanised rubber mould is produced. The process requires specialised equipment and highly skilled craftsmen, hence the varying quality of the products on the market. From this circular rubber mould, which is able to resist very high temperatures, the parts of the kit are produced. In the centre of this two-piece mould is a pouring hole. The mould is placed in a chamber which rotates;

molten metal is then poured into the centre, being distributed into the various parts of the mould by centrifugal force. Cooling is rapid; once removed from the chamber the mould is opened and the casting sprues are removed. It is genuinely a highly skilled operation, and those familiar with white metal figures will appreciate the craftsmanship involved. The products of, for example, John Tassel of Sovereign - who produces both white metal figures and AFVs - are of outstanding quality. Many of the resin producers also adopt white metal for the smaller parts; this is far more cost effective. However, the necessary skills are sometimes lacking, resulting in poor quality white metal parts. Since this is one of the hardest materials a modeller will encounter, remedial action is often very difficult. The three specific producers of white metal kits mentioned above are all high quality manufacturers.

All white metal parts should initially be cleaned up with a brass suede brush; this will remove many of the small surface impurities. For example, the talcum powder frequently used as a release agent by the producers leaves the surface of the metal with microscopic pit holes, which the brass brush will remove. Mould lines will demand more traditional treatment with blade, file or wetordry paper. The silicon rubber discs are the ideal means to achieve a mirror-like surface. Given sufficient pressure they will even cut the metal, but if used gently they can remove the mould lines with no adjacent damage.

A combination of glues is normally essential in working with white metal. If you are attaching small white metal details to each other, or small items to large, then super-glue is sufficient. However, the weight of bismuth alloy with its 58% lead content can produce problems in the long run, with weight distortion a distinct possibility. If the joint has to support weight then either solder with low melt solder or use an epoxy two-part glue. If white metal forms part of your resin kit then consider the installation of a discreet vertical brass support rod to take the load of the model and distribute it to the surface. Placed in the centre of the undercarriage, this can save a lot of remedial work in a year or two. (For the technique of low melt soldering, see Chapter Six.) As with any completed model, wash it thoroughly in soapy water before preparing to paint.

SUPER-DETAILING

This is arguably the most important facet of modelling to develop and master. The progression from super-detailing to conversions and scratch-building is evolutionary; indeed, for a competent super-detailer there is no hard division between these techniques. Super-detailing is required

Below
Some of the etched brass elements installed on Dragon's StuG kit.

Examples of Model Kasten's individual track links - expensive, but technically the best on the market. Dragon always, and Tamiya sometimes provide individual track links with their kits, but in the author's opinion Model Kasten's standard of detailing is superior.

on all high quality models, whether plastic, resin or scratch-built. To assist the modeller there are a substantial number of available accessories and tools. The first section which follows covers those accessories that are normally geared to a specific vehicle.

Etched metal

Since Tamiya re-entered the German AFV market about six years ago the quality of their kits has reached an excellent standard; they could literally be constructed without any additions. However, the limitations of kit production methods always invite some super-detailing. The fine mesh on engine louvres, clasps on tools, machine gun ring sights etc., are all examples of details too fine for mass production to the quality demanded by serious modellers.

Although used by model railway enthusiasts for many years, etched brass is an innovation for the AFV modeller. If I were to be asked to name the single reason for the general improvement in model quality over the last few years, I would choose etched brass. Photo-etching is a technique using both photography and chemical milling to produce fine detail. The most common metals used are copper, brass or nickel silver. Basically, a drawing is produced at a specific large scale. From this is made a high contrast film positive, reduced to the correct scale, with all the images of the items in black. The metal is coated with light-sensitive chemical; the film is applied to the metal; then the film is exposed to light so that the images are transferred to the metal. The metal is then subjected to an etching acid that erodes away those parts not protected by the light-sensitive chemical. (This is obviously a very simplified description of the technique.) It is possible to undertake your own etching, though this is something that I have not personally tried, as the prices for most commercial etched brass sets in England are reasonable.

While a number of kit manufacturers now include etched sets within their kits, there are really only three main quality etched set producers in the German AFV market: *On The Mark* from the USA, *The Show*

Modelling from Japan, and *Eduard* from the Czech Republic. On the Mark first appeared in the late 1980s and took the market by storm. In 1990 they brought out etched sets which covered the Panther and Tiger series, matching the old Nichimo and Tamiya kits. For some reason their product range has stagnated, with no new sets to cover the proliferation of Dragon, Italeri and Tamiya kits. Rather generous in size for the smaller scale items, they are nevertheless of good quality, with easy-to-follow instructions. Expensive for the larger Panther/Tiger in England, but cheap in the USA, they are well worth considering by the modeller who has a cupboard full of old Tamiya and Nichimo kits.

The Show Modelling from Japan are the most prolific of all the etched producers. Their range of products - while neither exclusively German nor etched sets - is extensive and of exceptionally high quality. Literally within a month or two of a new release from one of the plastic kit manufacturers The Show Modelling produce an etched set to complement or improve the kit. A range of over 80 sets combined with outstandingly fine detail makes these a pleasure to use. Sometimes indifferent instructions cause a degree of frustration, although for the items of fine detail additional parts are thoughtfully given.

Since the collapse of the Soviet Bloc we have been able to purchase products from some of the former Iron Curtain countries, among which Czechoslovakia always had the highest reputation for industrial sophistication. Eduard, a firm in the Czech Republic, has a large range of etched sets with approximately twenty German WWII subjects. Though not of a standard to rival The Show Modelling they are certainly very good value for money; and as they do not always directly overlap the range of their Japanese competitor they do provide some unique sets for the modeller.

Accurate Armour, while not providing etched sets for a specific vehicle, produce an invaluable range of etched floor plates; measuring about 150mm x 100mm, they are of excellent quality and at £6.00 represent good value for money.

One of the main uses of etched sets is to replace detail moulded onto plastic parts. Removing the original moulding is generally the hardest part of the operation; while it is fairly easy to remove plastic clasps from a shovel handle, this is not the case with, for example, jack restraints and frames. I would seriously consider remaking items like jacks and fire extinguishers before attempting to remove clasps from the moulded parts. With tool handles the easiest method is simply to cut the whole handle off and replace it with either plastic or brass rod. The remaking of detail is sometimes the only option if etched brass is to be incorporated into the model. Even etched brass itself may need detailing. The technique of etching is only capable of producing detail in two dimensions; in the case of e.g. hinges, the modeller will need to recreate the circular section of the hinge itself.

The use of etched sets requires a special finesse. The parts are invariably very small and difficult to handle - expect to spend a fair proportion of your modelling time in that familiar kneeling position on the carpet. The basic tools required are a sharp knife, a ceramic tile, high quality tweezers and pliers, and possibly a soldering set and heat source to anneal the metal. If the metal simply has to be removed from the fret and applied to the kit then the technique is straightforward. Place the fret on the ceramic tile and support the detail to be removed with your tweezers. Using a new knife blade, cut the item from its runner; if you do not support the part then it will spring into the air. You may need to clean up the edge where you removed it from the fret; the safest way is to hold the detail in your pliers, with the majority of it held within the jaws and only the section requiring cleaning exposed. Use a slitting abrasive disc in your motor tool, at a slow speed, to produce a clean straight edge. Filing or sanding of small detail carries the risk of bending or distortion. Once prepared, a small drop of super-glue (I use instant) is applied to the point of contact, and the part is placed in position with tweezers. If your glue is not instant then you may need to support the part temporarily. The main idea is to stick the metal to the model, however tenuously. Once this is achieved additional super-glue can be applied to obtain a strong joint. Do not overdo the super-glue, otherwise the whole point of etched brass - the fine detail - will be obliterated.

The common materials used in etched sets are brass and nickel silver, both of them hard with little ability to bend. This can be redressed by the application of heat (annealing). If the metal is heated to a high temperature and then quenched in water the strength is substantially reduced, making bending easy and rendering feasible shapes which would otherwise be impossible. I use a propane modelling torch; this requires careful application, as the temperature generated can be very high - on occasion my etched detail has melted before my eyes.... If any degree of strength is required in the joint then I solder it (see Chapter Six). The only point to remember if soldering is not to remove all the detail from the fret beforehand. Leave the main item on the fret, clean it with steel wool, and solder the other detail to the main component. Modelling of fine detail is more about ease of handling than anything else. A piece of Blue-tac attaching the main fret to your work bench will ensure rigidity while soldering. Small etched detail that requires a number of parts to be glued together is best achieved by gluing one part to the model and then adding to it. Once again, you are handling a large object, i.e. the tank, to which you are attaching detail. Trying to attach three or four small detached items together is a recipe for frustration and disaster.

Individual track links

The techniques for the installation of individual tracks have been described above; this passage covers only the products available to the modeller. *Model Kasten* remain the best, although expensive; no other manufacturer approaches the detail given in their tracks. The tendency to provide working tracks in their latest releases I find puzzling, as I would consider static models and dioramas the main market for their products. These working tracks are beautifully engineered and represent a kit within a kit. *Dragon, Tamiya* and *Academy* all offer individual track links, either as integral parts of the AFV kit or as optional extras to their vinyl tracks. Both *Accurate Armour* and *Cromwell* offer separate sets of resin tracks, either individual links or lengths, including some very interesting options, e.g. with Ostketten/snow grousers.

White metal tracks are increasingly being used by the "cottage industry". They require far less cleaning up than other materials, and do not suffer the same problems of quality control in production. However, they present particular problems in installation. The easiest way to install any type of individual track links is to make up and fit the correct length from drive sprocket to rear idler. Neither resin nor plastic present problems; once installed they can be bent or adjusted for track sag. White metal is more problematic. Super-glue does not provide the strength necessary to allow controlled bending for sag after fitting. I therefore solder the links together before installation. To achieve this without melting the white metal I use a low temperature solder and a pyrogravure, which gives a low,

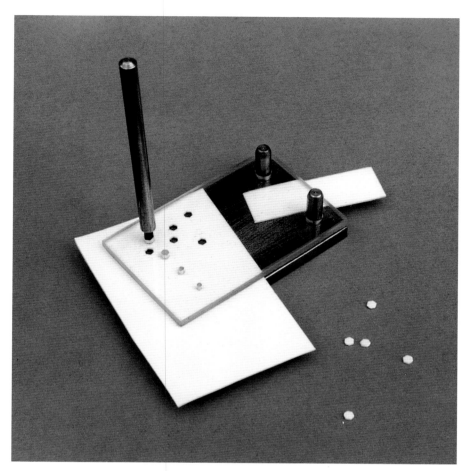

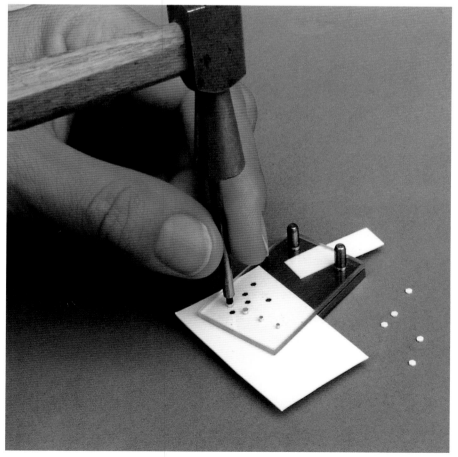

Above right

Historex Agents' punch and die kit set up for use - an invaluable aid to the super-detailer, converter and scratch-builder. Note the temporary plastic spacer on the right, which ensures that the two halves of the set are level, protecting it against needless wear and damage.

Right

A small modelling hammer is also required. Try to restrict use of the punch and die set to plastic; brass and aluminium will quickly wear out the punch heads. Do not hit too hard - a gentle tap is usually enough, even with fairly thick (20/1000) plastic.

controllable heat. Once soldered the joins are sufficiently strong to allow bending after installation on the tank. The bottom run of tracks are also soldered, with the links used individually only around the drive sprocket and idler.

Friulmodellismo of Italy provide individual track links which remain flexible once joined. A jig is provided, unique to each type of track, which enables lengths of links to be joined. Highly detailed, these are expensive; but they have the advantage that no artificial sag is required, the metal links hanging realistically under their own weight. Keeping them flexible presents some problems during priming and painting, however; I would recommend that once correctly positioned they are glued in place. Avoid handling them during finishing phases; they have a tendency to become flexible again, and accumulations of super-glue do nothing for the appearance of the finished model.

Gun barrels

Most plastic kits provide the modeller with the barrel in two halves; "high tech" kits with a lathe-turned aluminium barrel; and resin kits with a resin tube. Apart from the lathe-turned barrel these can present problems. The plastic barrels require careful work to remove mould lines; resin barrels frequently resemble lethal bananas, and are very difficult to correct. Immersion in boiling water and rolling with the palm of your hand on a perfectly flat surface can sometimes correct the smaller lengths, but longer barrels are very difficult to straighten. Fortunately a Spanish company, *Jordy Rubio*, has come to the rescue with a high quality, reasonably priced range of German and Soviet barrels, covering the main calibres, in lathe-turned aluminium.

Headlights

While most Wehrmacht vehicles had slotted blackout covers on their nightime lights, these were often removed when out of the front line. To recreate the brightness of a headlight is very simple. You can either buy purpose-made lights, or you can make your own; either way you will need to drill out the centre of the light. I normally use the tip of the hobby knife to indent the centre of the headlight,and a dental burr to ream out the concave shape required. If you have a source of clear epoxy resin then this is the cheapest option. First ensure a smooth background to the plastic; then paint the inside of the light with a high gloss silver - I would recommend Tamiya's enamel paint marker pen, as this chrome silver is the brightest on the market. After drying, mix up a sufficient quantity of clear resin. Place the headlight in a piece of Blue-tac, perfectly level. With a cocktail stick very carefully fill the headlight up with resin and leave to cure; try to fill from the centre of the recess, so that strings do not touch the sides. After the initial cure any surplus can be carefully removed with a clean cocktail stick. For the lazier modeller MV Products from the USA have a substantial range of both head and rear lights, in clear resin with a silvered back; price depends on the diameter. I use Elmers white glue for installation; this safe children's glue dries completely flat and invisible, and takes a few minutes to dry, allowing exact positioning. Should any glue

get onto the lens it can be wiped off with water.

Miscellaneous accessories

There are surprisingly few companies which supply replacement/improvement parts; the majority of accessories relate to conversions. One of my favourites is *Cornerstone Models* in the USA, who supply a very accurate, highly detailed range of resin engines, gearboxes and transmissions for most marks of German tanks; newer releases include radios and MG cartridge bags. *Model Kasten* is also found in this field, with a range of tank/halftrack wheels and many other items of miscellaneous tank equipment. Injection moulding techniques ensure the very highest quality. Tiger wheels are provided for early, mid-war and late versions. For the purist they are the ultimate in accuracy, though rather expensive. Another Japanese company, *Clipper Models*, have a growing range principally geared to the improvement of Dragon kits; these range from buffer sets through vehicle jacks to barrels, using white metal, resin and etched metal. Clipper Models offer a very interesting and exceptionally high quality range of products. Regrettably, due to high labour costs and the power of the Japanese currency, most products from that country appear to be very expensive. However, those prepared to pay the price are rarely disappointed with Japanese goods.

Perhaps the newest manufacturer is *New Connection Models* from Germany, who offer to date an expanding range of high quality resin and white metal conversions - and also a series of figures sculpted by Stefan Müller Herdemertens (see Chapter Eight). *Verlinden's* prolific output includes a number of items to improve models, ranging from engines to radios. His very high quality castings, although not always user-friendly, are probably the best value for money on the market. *The Show Modelling*, while principally an etched set company, do produce some items for the super-detailer including jacks, Bosch headlights and fire extinguishers. Casting is by the "lost wax" technique used in the production of jewellery; the material is brass, and provided the item is free of blemishes you have the hardest material you are likely to encounter in your modelling. Should cleaning be necessary this can only be achieved with files and wetdry paper. They have also recently produced a set of plastic injection moulded Opel Blitz wheels, highly detailed and good value for money.

There are of course many other manufacturers who provide miscellaneous details for the modeller; regrettably most of these products are plagiarised from their original makers (all too easy for the unscrupulous), and I do not intend to give publicity to such companies.

* * *

The foregoing section covers the main accessories that can be purchased, generally orientated to a specific vehicle/model. The comments which follow cover techniques and tools enabling you to manufacture your own super-detail.

The single tool which has most radically improved my detailing is my **punch and die set**. There are only two worth considering on the market: *Historex Agents* sell round and

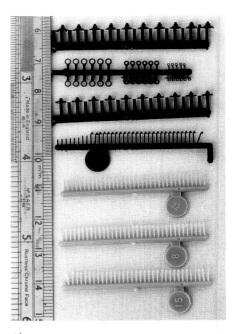

Above
Examples of Grandt Line nuts and bolts. Note how the new grey colour makes these beautiful little components difficult to see, compared with the black plastic formerly used.

hexagonal types, and *Waldron* sell two round sets offering a greater choice of diameter. The Historex sets retail for around £30.00 each, Waldron's for about $120.00 dollars for the two sets. Both manufacturers' products are superbly engineered precision tools, and both work in an identical manner. The die is a two-piece mould; the bottom half is of steel with a number of precise vertical holes drilled through. Two locating pins in the steel die secure a repeat clear perspex die on top, the holes through both matching exactly. A series of punches which exactly match the diameters of the holes enable materials of varying thickness to be punched out. Hence the main use is producing countless numbers of either very small rivets of different depths, or circular shapes up to the largest punch diameter. Plastic card is the recommended material to use - which, being soft, gives the set a limitless life; it will also punch through brass sheet, but the use of metals will wear down the edges of both punch and die. When punching through the plasticard ensure that the steel and perspex halves of the device are parallel, i.e. level. Do not punch your strip of plastic without ensuring that the two parts of the die are balanced; if necessary place another piece of plastic at the other end of the die to level it up. If you do not adopt this technique then over a short space of time the edges of both punch and die will become rounded, and bolts will appear with furry edges; while a new edge can be ground onto the punch, once the edge of the die is lost then your set is up for replacement.

Instrument panels

Do not at first cut out the exact shape of the panel. On a piece of 0.5mm plasticard mark out the overall shape and the positions of the dials. After punching out the dials, cut the panel to size and shape. From a piece of 0.25mm card, punch out discs of the same diameter as the dials; insert these in the holes and glue. You should now paint the instrument panel. Using 0.25mm clear plastic, punch out further discs to match those in the dials and place in the recessed holes. The fit will be tight enough not to need gluing.

Recessed bolt holes

From your piece of plasticard punch out the required number of bolt holes. Glue a piece of thinner card to the back of the main piece. Punch out bolts of the same diameter as the holes but of a thinner card; using the punch, insert these into the punched holes and glue. Even recessed screw heads can be made by this method. Repeat all the procedures, but instead of making bolts of the exact diameter choose the next size down; I would suggest punching out the number required plus 20% for wastage. Cut each tiny disc in half; carefully insert each half in the recessed bolt hole, making sure the "slots" of the screw heads are parallel, and glue in position.

Miscellaneous bolts, screws & rivets

Normal bolts can be made in their thousands, and I generally make many more than I need - I usually manage to lose a huge number. Store the bolts on a piece of dark material. By the nature of the punch, one side of each bolt will be very slightly domed; before positioning them turn the bolts over so that the dome is uppermost. If a row of bolts is to be installed then on the card mark out the position of every bolt in pencil. Use your best tweezers to pick and place. After positioning approximately five, use a plastic glue to seal them in position, adjusting the bolts before the plastic cures. Repeat till complete. Even if you are gluing plastic to metal you can use the same technique; the plastic of the bolts will become sufficiently soft to bond temporarily to the metal, and you can follow up with super-glue applied with a fine wire. Be careful not to swamp the detail by overdoing the super-glue.

While the punch and die set enables either round or hexagonal shapes to be produced, you will often require specific nut and bolt heads. When these heads are very small the eye can be deceived by using the punch and die set. From the model railway hobby one manufacturer comes to our aid - *Grandt Line* from the United States. They have a vast product range for the railway enthusiast, including a series of nuts, bolts, lifting eyes, hinges etc. in injection moulded plastic. The number of items supplied varies with the size; with the smallest bolts we receive approximately 175 bolts in a single packet for less than $2.00. One of the drawbacks is the bewildering variety of scales and imperial measurements used in the catalogues. Thus the size of one bolt in imperial and at a particular scale is found to be the same item

at a different imperial size and scale; so repetitious purchases can be a problem. Once these items were produced in a black plastic which was relatively easy to see, but for some inexplicable reason they now produce these minute pieces in a light grey plastic.

The easiest way to install them is to cut the bolt head from the sprue, position and glue. In order to cut the bolt head free you obviously need to cut at 90 degrees to the line of the sprue. If this is not achieved then the bolt head will not sit perfectly level in its final position. This is not as easy as it sounds, and the difficulty is compounded by the light grey plastic. I have no solution to the poor visibility of the plastic other than to use an optical magnifier. For removal from the sprue I place the sprue on a piece of plasticard, thicker than the diameter of the bolt heads, and with the bolts hanging over the edge I run the knife blade up the shank until it stops at the bolt. Provided the blade is new a clean cut is assured. Pick the bolts up with your best tweezers, and position; apply plastic glue

sparingly, as you do not want to destroy the fine detail. Before the plastic cures move the bolts into their final and exact position. (If you are a regular user of Grandt Line you might consider writing to them and requesting that they revert to black plastic!)

Beading tools (grainers)

These are rather similar in use to the punch and die set but lacking the finesse. Regrettably, the technique requires some rather specialised accessories: a piece of vulcanised rubber and printer's aluminium sheet, neither of which are easy to obtain, especially the vulcanised rubber. Casters of white metal figures are the only source that I know; you might find out which manufacturers use these vulcanised rubber moulds, and write to them asking if you can purchase a worn-out mould when they are about to throw it away. This rubber is extremely dense and yet still pliable. Using the rubber as backing for a thin piece of

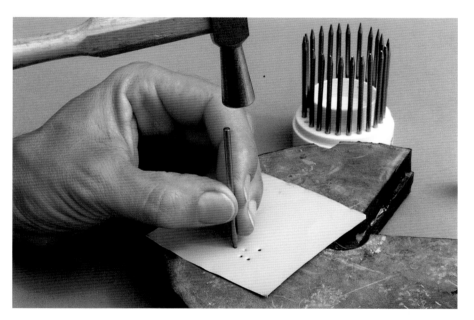

Right
Beading tool/grainer in use, punching domed rivet heads out of a scrap piece of printer's aluminium sheet against a backing pad of waste vulcanised rubber. Good quality tweezers are essential to extract the tiny discs from the rubber.

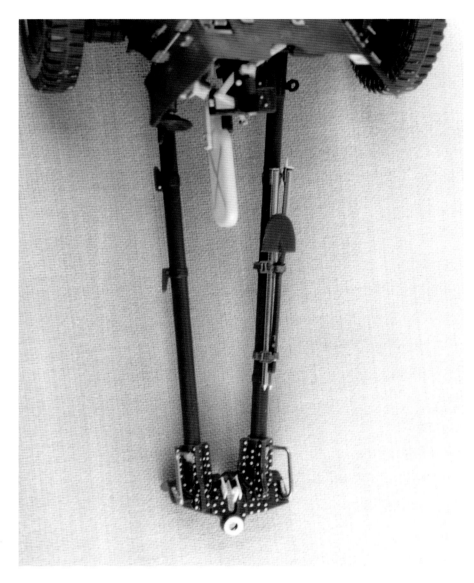

of rivets. Check that the grainer is in contact with the steel edge. Run the grainer along the rule, gently tapping the rivet shapes. The method for plastic is very similar, but the grainers will distort the plastic after punching. You therefore need to indent the rivets before you cut the main component shape from the plasticard. Mark out the overall shape and the position of the rivets. Form the rivets; then on the underside of the plastic sand off the protruding indent shape. Once complete, cut the shape from the card.

Rough-cast texture

Despite Germany's limited mineral resources she developed the most sophisticated steel armour of the last war; even near final defeat the quality of the steel was unimpaired. It is therefore a total misconception to alter the texture of German plastic kits to the degree that we sometimes observe on some modellers' vehicles; all marks of vehicles up to the Panzerkampfwagen IV had a clean, smooth appearance to the steel. Only on the thickest armour, i.e. the glacis plate of Panthers and Tigers, do we find a distinct texture to the surface, though this is still smooth in comparison to that found on the turrets of the Soviet T-34 and KV-1 series, for instance. On many plastic kits the surface texture provided is quite sufficient; however, Tigers and Panthers do need a gentle application of rough-cast. The normal way is to coat the surface liberally with plastic glue, wait a few minutes, and then stab the surface with a stiff brush. I do not support this method myself, but prefer to use mechanical means. I use firstly the smallest stone-setting burr (1.00 mm diameter) in my motor drill. Set the slowest speed; place the drill body in the palm of your hand; and allow the burr to bounce on the surface of the plastic. Do not force the burr into the plastic; allow it to travel aimlessly around the surface. Remove this burr and replace it with the smallest round ball burr (0.5 mm diameter); repeat the process, ensuring that all areas are covered.

Once you are satisfied, clean the plastic with 0000 gauge steel wool to ensure that there is no plastic residue left standing proud. Dragon kits occasionally use a plastic that seems impervious to the steel wool - the Maus is an example of a vehicle that does need a texture applied generally all over. I had problems cleaning up with the wool. In this case I resorted to the plastic glue. Do not use a small brush, use a wide flat sable - you have only one pass. If you go over the plastic again before the plastic has cured you will put brush marks into it. After curing, restore the matt effect with the steel wool. Remember, do not over-texture.

Weld seams

The welds joining the steel plates had equally superior characteristics; before you enhance

aluminium you can stamp out thousands of concave discs. The grainers come in a 20-piece set from 0.3 mm to 1.25 mm diameter. The heads are concave and therefore produce domed discs when used with the rubber.

If you do manage to obtain the vulcanised rubber and printer's aluminium sheet then this technique is within your grasp. To manufacture the very smallest bolts/rivets you only additionally need the smallest round burr. With pliers snap off the burr head; this should leave a pointed tool, whose head you may need to flatten with a slitting disc - you should end up with a punch, diameter approximately 0.4 mm. With a small modeller's hammer punch out the tiny bolts/rivets from the aluminium; these will be indented into the rubber, and domed; you will need your best quality tweezers and a magnifying aid to extract them from the rubber and invert them. They can be applied to either plastic or non-plastic surfaces. Mark out their position exactly with a pencil and metal ruler; position them with the tweezers and set them with plastic glue, using the tweezers to push them into the surface. Provided you do not excessively handle the model the rivets should remain in position until finally sealed by the primer and subsequent paint finishes.

Should I apply these bolts to a non-plastic surface then I use a slightly different method. Mark out the positions as before. You will need two 00 gauge paint brushes. Instead of glue, use the finest quality artist's gloss varnish - I use varnish with the consistency of water. Apply with one brush to the general area. Moisten the tip of the other with your lips and use it to pick up and position a single bolt. Repeat, making sure that you do not pick up any varnish; if you do then the bolts will not leave the brush. If this happens clean the brush with white spirit. After you have completed a line, leave the varnish to dry before giving the area with the bolts another coat of varnish. Once again, this method is sufficiently strong provided the model is not handled excessively.

You can also use the grainers to impress into plastic or metal the circumference of a disc; this is another way of producing flush rivets. You do need to take a few precautions with this method. If you are using brass or aluminium then no special measures are needed. Clean the metal with steel wool; this will enable you to mark in pencil the exact position of each rivet. Using either Blue-tac or tape, attach a metal ruler parallel to the line

Right
Figs.1 & 2: The two methods of reproducing weld seams, as described in the text.

any weld lines study photographs of the real vehicle. I use two methods, both of them simple and effective. To enhance existing weld lines you only need the tools mentioned above for rough-cast texturing, plus some insulating tape. The tape should be accurately positioned either side of the weld joint; insulating tape is better for this job than Selotape in that it is thicker and stronger - should the burr in the drill slip then the insulating tape will protect the adjacent area (see accompanying drawing, Fig.1). Use the stone-setting burr first, engraving at 90 degrees to the line of the seam; once this is complete change to the round burr and repeat. When you are satisfied with the degree of detail, clean with steel wool or carefully wipe with plastic glue.

The second method is especially effective. Using a plastic scribing cutter (P-cutter), scribe a line along the length of the required weld; due to the shape of the blade this will cut a V- section. Once sufficient depth has been scribed, take a piece of spare round sprue and heat it over a flame, stretching it until you have a sufficient length of the right diameter. Cut the sprue to the weld length and test it in the V-cut. If the right amount of sprue is exposed, then plastic glue in position; if not, cut a deeper groove and try again. Apply super-glue to the joint on either side of the weld; do not overfill - applying with a fine piece of wire gives good control. Once the plastic has cured repeat the burring and cleaning steps as above (see Fig.2). Should very heavy seams be required - a rarity on German vehicles - then use Milliput, and leave for approximately one hour before recreating the weld seams with a fine point spatula.

Restraint should be the watchword when either texturing plates or enhancing welds - do not forget the quality of German steel. You can always go back and increase the texturing; replacing excessive finishes is not so easy.

Stretched sprue

While round section plastic rod can be found in most model shops, there are occasions when particular diameters are not available. The easiest way to obtain the exact size is to use the technique of stretched sprue - spare plastic sprue is heated over a naked flame and then literally stretched to the desired length and diameter. A point to consider is that the cross section of the stretched filament will mimic the original shape of the sprue: e.g. an elliptical section piece of plastic will stretch to a thinner but still basically elliptical shape. If you want perfectly round sprue, then use perfectly round sprue. (You can of course stretch commercial plastic rod.) Do not allow the sprue or rod to catch fire; not only will you be unable to stretch it, but cyanide gas is given off. The thinner the diameter required, the greater the heat: if you want larger diameters then either restrict the heat or allow the sprue to cool. Pull in opposite directions until the required diameter is obtained, then allow to cool for a few seconds before cutting to length. I do not use stretched sprue for aerials; I am much too clumsy to avoid breaking the delicate plastic filament during

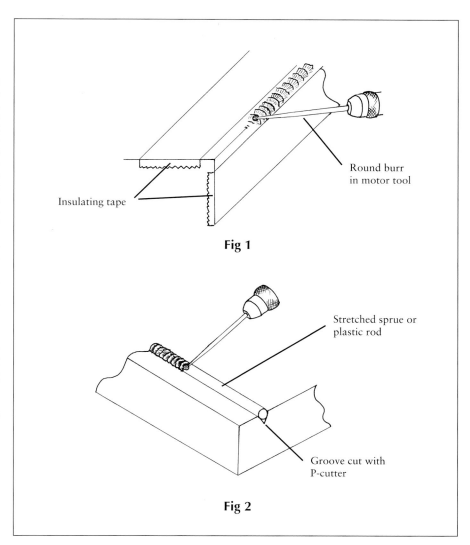

Fig 1

Insulating tape

Round burr in motor tool

Fig 2

Stretched sprue or plastic rod

Groove cut with P-cutter

Below
Given the quality of most wartime German steel plate, reproducing a rough-cast finish should seldom be necessary. Where it is appropriate, allow your drill to "bounce" in the palm of your hand while the burr skips over the surface; do not apply pressure to the burr or it will dig deep ruts in the plastic. After covering all necessary surfaces, clean them with fine steel wool (gauge 0000).

construction or painting, so I always use fine stiff steel wire.

Lead foil

Lead offers many advantages to the modeller. It can be purchased in a variety of sheet thicknesses; I personally use 0.2mm sheet bought from *Scale Link*. A large sheet costing only a few pounds should last you many years. Thicker sheet can be obtained from medical suppliers; and there is always the ubiquitous wine bottle top (but the vintage needs to be good - these days the tendency is for plastic or tin sheet). The beauty of lead is its softness and malleability. It will contort to any shape required, and once moulded it will retain this position; and it can be cut with scissors or a surgical blade.

Do not try to form the required shape away from its final permanent position. Cut to length; using super-glue, attach only one part of the lead. Once the glue is dry (a matter of seconds) you can shape the remainder of the lead to its final position and glue it in place. I tend to use lead for two main purposes: as fine straps, or as damaged thin metal, e.g. side skirts, mudguards, stowage bins, etc. If you intend to use lead for mudguards do not use the very thin sheet; 0.5mm is more suitable. It is very easy to damage lead sheet by excessive

Left
The two methods of reproducing weld seams were both employed on this scratch-built Panther II turret - simple burring around the edges of the roof, and "cut and fill" along the rear edge of the massive front plate.

handling, and I would leave this detailing until a late stage. Battle damage should be applied in moderation; excessive damage looks unrealistic. Small arms fire can be recreated with a needle pushed through the lead, as can small tears.

Remember that lead must be primed; unprimed lead will suffer oxidisation over a period of time, leading to the condition dreaded among figure modellers as "lead cancer" - your paint will start to powder off, by which time a general deterioration of the lead will already be well under way. All metal detail on your models should be primed, whether, copper, brass, lead or alloys.

Clasps, buckles and dial rims

On occasion we sometimes need substantial numbers of these items; while many etched sets provide them, it is sometimes just as easy to make your own. In the section on punch and die tools I described how to make an instrument panel; but what if the dials had raised rims? How can you make hundreds of tiny square/rectangular clasps, or individual chain links? This technique is a lot simpler than you might think, and the standard is only dependant on the quality of the form that you use.

If you want to make tiny rectangular clasps,

for instance, you will need a solid rectangular brass section slightly smaller than the shape you wish to construct. These sections are available from a number of hobby shops in Britain, but the most comprehensive distributor is *John Flack*. You can buy any structural shape you wish, from I- and T-beams to L- and U- sections; and they are available in the most minute sizes (square sections down to 1x1mm!).

You can buy a wide variety of diameters of copper wire; firm yet pliable, this can be cut with a hobby knife. Your wire may have been wrapped around a small diameter drum; it is easier to work with straight wire, and the most successful way to straighten it is to put it under tension. Put one end in a vice and hold the other end in your pliers; apply gentle pulling power - not too much, or it may snap.

To make your clasps or other shapes, put one end of the brass former in the vice and begin tightly wrapping the copper wire around it. Once you have sufficient for your needs, place the brass on a ceramic tile, temporarily supporting the ends on two pieces of plastic taped to the tile. With an industrial

Below
Lead sheet cut and shaped for the rear muffler guards on Tamiya's Königstiger. It is also much easier to reproduce battle damage realistically by using lead foil than by trying to pierce or distort the kit's plastic parts.

razor held parallel to the brass former, and a hammer, sever the links of the copper. You will now have countless perfect outline shapes in copper (you will need to flatten them individually on the tile). All shapes are possible by this method, governed purely by the section of brass former. It is essential that the material of the former is very hard, otherwise the shape will be distorted when you sever the wire spiral into links.

Width indicator gauges

Virtually all German softskins and many AFVs had these "feeler" gauges to warn drivers if they were about to attempt passing through too narrow a gap. They were simply narrow, sometimes single, tapered or telescopic rods with a white painted ball at the end which indicated the maximum vehicle width; generally fitted on the front mudguards, they were visible to the driver.

There are a number of ways to tackle these gauges. The easiest is to purchase them from *The Show Modelling*, who sell pairs of turned brass gauges for a few pounds. I use a combination of these and ones I make myself; the brass examples are fairly short and are not suitable for all subjects, and making them is easy with the correct materials.

The main ingredient is a selection of hypodermic needles; you can buy a variety of diameters from your local chemist or drug store, and the hollow stainless steel needles have endless uses for the modeller. In addition to any telescopic items (they frequently fit within each other) they make superb machine gun barrels. For the width indicators you only need a piece of fine wire to insert into the tube. The globe at the end is fashioned by mixing up a small quantity of epoxy glue, and applying it to the end of the indicator with a piece of wire. Hold the indicator vertically with the blob of glue at the bottom, and rotate it; if the glue is disproportionally applied to one side, gently blow on it until it is even. Stick a bit of Blue-tac under your work bench and carefully position the indicator hanging perfectly vertical; when the glue is dry you should have a perfect globe at the end of the rod. (Although most epoxy glues dry in ten minutes they will not tolerate handling for one or two hours; be patient, or you may destroy the shape of the globe.) Drill a fine hole in the mudguard; place your gauge in the hole, checking that the angle is correct and the position represents the width of the vehicle; and glue in place.

Towing and track cables

Like all AFVs, German vehicles carried towing cables, and the larger types, e.g. Tigers, track cables. The sheer weight of the tracks made it impossible for the crew to manhandle the links into place without the help of the Tiger's power plant. The track cables were attached to the drive sprocket and the track; the sprocket was turned and the track slowly pulled forward over the wheels until it could be connected to the bottom run of the tracks.

Most plastic kits provide moulded towing cables; I generally use the towing eye, but always replace the cable. I do not use any one single material for this, but generally make them from brass or nylon; picture framing brass wire is ideal for the larger tanks, if annealed (see above under Etched Metal) to

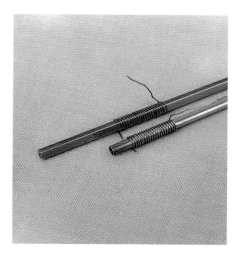

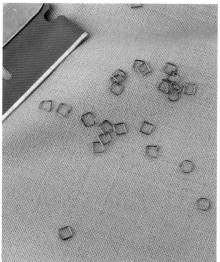

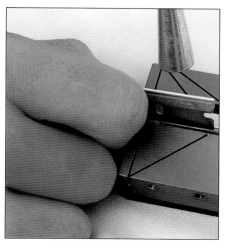

Top left
Copper wire wrapped tightly around a specific brass shape - square and circular, in this case - provides the basis for tiny clasps, buckles and dial rims.

Top right
The brass shape is firmly clasped in a jig, and the wire spiral is severed into individual links using an industrial razor. This is essentially the same method used on a larger scale by ancient armourers to make ring-mail.

Left
The result: many perfectly formed squares and rings.

allow easier bending and positioning. Nylon is also very useful, as it is totally pliable and will contort to any shape. Do not use cotton, whose many fine fibres will be highlighted when subsequently dry-brushed. If you are forced to use the cotton then paint it first with white glue - this should seal the fine hairs.

Once you have decided on the cable material, cut the towing eye from the plastic cable. Clean it thoroughly (it will be dry-brushed later); and with your knifepoint indent the end exactly in the middle. With a drill bit of similar diameter to the cable, drill out the shank of the towing eye to a depth of at least 4mm or 5mm. Insert the new cable, and seal with super-glue. If you use nylon you will need to seal the ends with heat or super-glue to prevent it unravelling. Check the length carefully before fitting the eye to the other end.

I cannot recommend any substitute other than making the track cables yourself. For this I use four strands of unlacquered 0.2mm copper wire. Cut four identical lengths, approximately 450mm; twist one end and clamp in a vice. Make a loop at the other end and attach (preferably) to a hand drill, but if necessary to a motor drill; you will only need one or two seconds with a motor drill or a little longer by hand. If the copper is unlacquered you can easily turn one end into a loop and solder it into an eye. Before

making them you should study the exact direction and length of the stowed track cables; you will need very precise measurements to loop the free end to engage exactly with the locating pin on the hull side.

*　　*　　*

Every serious modeller will accumulate substantial quantities of plastic, brass and other sheet and strip materials; the available permutations would appear to be endless. They are indispensable to the modeller; and a fuller description of the manufacturers and products will be found in the next chapter on conversions and scratch-building.

CHAPTER FIVE
CONVERSION & SCRATCH-BUILDING

The term "conversion" covers two approaches to modelling: either purchasing a commercial conversion kit, together with the master kit to be adapted; or undertaking the alteration yourself.

Commercial conversion products

As mentioned already, the publication *Panzer File 94/95* illustrates the very substantial "cottage industry" which has sprung up in the past ten years to provide mostly conversions, but also full vehicle kits. Those companies described in Chapter Three as offering full resin kits are also the main contenders in the conversion market. Comments relating to accuracy and quality are equally relevant in this field.

In some ways it is more difficult to produce a resin conversion for a plastic kit than a full resin kit. Both RTV and resin suffer from shrinkage, and there would appear to be no exact science to accurately predict this reduction. The consensus is that the finished product will shrink by about 4% - a substantial amount on a large component. Accordingly, while the master may well fit exactly when offered up to the plastic kit, an allowance must be made for this shrinkage in production. Smaller resin components shrink at different rates from larger items, and these differential shrinkages are the cause of some of the problems besetting the "cottage industry" conversions. Most of the companies mentioned in Chapter Three have overcome this problem; and for those modellers who do not wish to undertake major scratch-building they offer a very acceptable alternative for producing non-standard vehicles not covered by the major injection moulding manufacturers.

If you intend to use a conversion kit then the first requirement will probably be to remove sections of the original plastic kit. Good conversion designers will have manufactured their products in a user-friendly way, so that the removal of existing sections is a straightforward task. I invariably use a power tool for this, usually a small circular steel saw, with the drill set at the slowest speed to avoid frictional heat - this can rapidly melt the plastic in and adjacent to the cut, locking the saw and making a mess which is difficult to clean up. Cut the plastic about 0.5mm - 1.0mm back from the final line. Corners can either be cut with a hand saw or a standard drill bit, which will obviously produce a rounded corner; a crisp 90 degree corner can later be restored with a file. Once the superfluous section has been removed you will need to clean up the edges of the remaining plastic to a smooth, level and (most importantly) straight line. To get within 0.5mm of the final line I use the largest and roughest file that can be used in the circumstances. It is a fallacy that because you are working in miniature the tools should

Above
Two set squares, running along each other, enable perfect parallel lines to be drawn, in this case on plastic sheet.

Left
Marked out on the plastic card is the base for a scratch-built Schmalturm to replace that provided in Dragon's Panther II kit. Note the double lines, making allowance for the thickness of plastic to be used for the side walls.

always be miniature. I learnt this lesson from the late Richard Almond, who made the most exquisite masters using tools that one would normally associate with jail breakouts! The art lies in using suitable implements for the job, and finishing with the finest tools; the skill and craftsmanship is in the hands, not the tools.

To achieve a straight, clean line when filing or sanding is sometimes very difficult. I tend to construct a purpose-made sanding block for the final operation. I have a 10mm wide steel rule to which I attach wetordry paper with double sided tape. For sanding jobs of lesser width I make up narrow sanding blocks in the same way but using plastic strip as the basis; these are never less than 3mm deep but the width will depend on the individual task. Attempting to sand down a 20mm wide gap with a sanding block only 5mm wide is asking for an uneven finish. Rectangular files will accurately restore the corners if necessary.

You may need to remove superfluous surface detail, hinges for example. The initial stage is best undertaken with a chisel blade in a hobby knife. Once I have cut down to the level of the

adjacent surface I again use purpose-made sanding blocks, but with a plastic stem glued at rightangles to the reverse as a grip; use a circular motion to give a smooth, level finish. Finally clean with 0000 gauge steel wool. Should the chisel slip and accidentally cut into the plastic, this is easily restored with super-glue sprinkled with baking powder (bicarbonate of soda), which produces a rock hard surface. Finish the surface of the powder with super-glue; if there is any residue left, then when the model is washed the baking powder will react with water, expand, and crystallise. The sanding process should be repeated until an acceptable finish is obtained.

For the stout-hearted modeller a more robust method of removing surface detail is to drill or cut out the item. On the underside of the hole glue a piece of plasticard that covers the aperture; fill the hole with Milliput, and bring to a smooth, level surface with a spatula and water. When the Milliput has cured, clean with wetordry and steel wool.

Depending upon location and strength requirements you will need to decide on the type of glue to use, either epoxy or super-glue.

Small resin/white metal parts can be initially attached to the main plastic kit part with ordinary plastic solvent. The glue will not affect the conversion parts but will soften the plastic for a few minutes, which should be adequate to position the part precisely; then follow up sparingly with instant super-glue. With instant glue the curing period can be briefly extended by applying it to both surfaces rather than one; this should give you maybe 30 seconds to manoeuvre and position precisely. For strength, hidden joints, or difficult-to-position joints use epoxy.

SCRATCH-BUILDS

Pure scratch-building - in which the modeller produces 100% of all components - is generally rare. The majority of models can be scratch-built using components of analogous kits. In many ways a extensive conversion can be more difficult than a pure scratch-build. Scratch-building demands little more than an aptitude for precise measurement and some technical skills; heavy conversions require a degree of compromise which is sometimes difficult to accept. You will frequently find errors and sometimes very substantial inaccuracies in existing kits; and you will have to decide whether to compromise on these errors, or to scratch-build.

As stressed in Chapter Two, the most important facet of scratch-building/conversions is to have good reference material. Just as most models contain errors, so do scale drawings. If you can get two

Below
The P-cutter and steel rule are used to scribe the snap line into the surface of the plastic card; then pliers are used to ensure a clean snap.

different sets of plans to agree then you are very lucky! Spend as much time as possible absorbing the assembled information and cross-referencing, until you have a set of plans or measurements of which you are confident. This may require the drawing of plans - rarely full drawings, but sections that may prove difficult to construct otherwise. The standard three views are not normally sufficient; isometric, oblique views are all very useful. It is now that those photographs of the subject provide the final understanding of the project.

Scale & measurement

Even if you have a set of plans in which you feel confident, check the scale. Paper shrinks and expands like most materials - and so will your plans. To check the accuracy of the scale requires a simple mathematical calculation. Virtually all plans stipulate the scale they are drawn at and include a scale marker. Ignore what scale they claim to be; measure and check the scale marker on the drawing. If your scale is meant to be 1:35, and the marker represents, for instance, four metres (4000mm) and measures 116mm: then the scale of the drawing is 4000mm divided by 116mm, i.e. 1:34.48. If you wish to build at 1:35 then you will need to make an adjustment to all measurements taken from the drawing. This is another simple calculation. Divide the actual scale, 34.48, by the required scale, 35. This will give you either a constant to put in your calculator (i.e. 98.5%) or, if you have the use of a photocopier with a precise zoom facility, the ability to alter the plans (i.e. reduce by 1.5%). If you use the calculator method then all measurements taken from the drawings will need to be adjusted by the calculated percentage.

You may also have drawings without any scale indicated on them; and this represents the greatest challenge. Unfortunately there appear to be no hard and fast rules which govern the measurement of vehicles. What is the length of a vehicle - is it between the tips of the front and rear mudguards? Is the height of a vehicle from the base of the tracks to the turret roof, or the commander's cupola? Without any specific rules we confront several differing measurements, all right in their own way. You should always try to use the longest measurement available; but the only measurement about which there seems to be little disagreement is the width. Example: the reference book gives the width of the tank as 3050mm. Your plan scales 84.75mm, therefore divide 3050mm by 84.75 to give the scale of the plans as 35.99, i.e. 1:36. Apply the correction to either the photocopier or the calculator as previously described.

What if the plans do not conform to the measurements of the model you have bought to be converted? That is when you must decide whether you wish to compromise, or to scrap the kit and scratch-build. If the decision is to compromise, then take one of the longest measurement on the vehicle, i.e. from the centre of the drive sprocket to the rear idler, and check the same measurement on the drawings; this will produce the ratio for you to adopt. Your plans should be adjusted so that the resultant conversion is in sympathy with the model you are converting.

Above
An adjustable metal protractor ensures that angles are correct before the glue sets; note that the scale plans are kept handy during the modelling process.

Example: the length on the model equals 140mm; the same length on the plan equals 136mm; and 140mm divided by 136mm equals 1.029. Therefore adjust all measurements taken from the plan by increasing them by 2.9%.

Finally, some photographs can also be used for measurement purposes, although with the greatest caution. I would not rely on major measurements using photographs, purely because the only truly accurate part of a photograph is in the centre of the picture; right and left of this point the image is distorted, and increasingly so towards the edges. However, I sometimes rely on my photographs to position minor detail. Example: to find the position of a bolt hole in a plate. You have measured the length of the plate to be 1450mm. In your photograph this measures 23mm; the bolt measures 6mm from the datum point, therefore its true distance from that point is 6 divided by 23 times 1450, equals 378mm. This is not foolproof, obviously, but it is a useful method of obtaining additional measurements in the absence of primary information.

Drawings

Hopefully you will not have to produce full plans; but you will certainly need to mark - either on paper or, more often, on plasticard - the shape that you have to cut out. Whilst I do have a full drawing set including board, parallels, T-square, etc., 90% of the time I only use a compass and two set squares. With 45 and 60/30 degree set squares you can produce perfect parallel lines. Use these squares only for drawing, never for cutting. By setting the two hypotenuses (the long sides) of the set squares together and sliding one upon the other you can produce these lines.

If you have to produce a shape only once then it is best if this is drawn directly onto the plastic card; it may be necessary to roughen the surface with 0000 gauge steel wool for the pencil to mark. For fine measurements I use a 0.3mm propelling pencil with an HB lead. Should I need multiple copies then the initial drawing is done on paper; once it is completed the paper is transferred to the plastic, and held firmly in position while each corner (or change in direction) is pricked through with the point of a compass. Line up the holes and

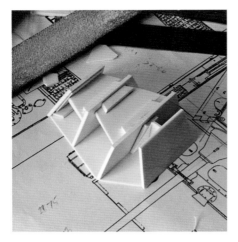

Above
The basic turret shape, with lots of miscellaneous plastic to support the side walls, mostly located at changes of angle or direction.

Above right
Copious quantities of super-glue and baking powder are used to strengthen the plastic joints and to enable continuous work to proceed.

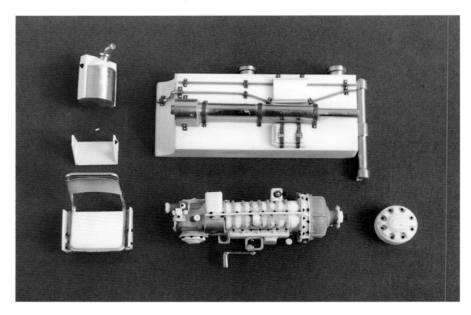

mark out the shape. With the set squares check that parallel lines are still correctly aligned. For non-rectangular/square shapes do not rely simply on length and width measurements, but also check diagonals. From the longest base line mark out the two ends and, using a compass, scribe the two arcs from one of these points, transfer to the other end and repeat. Join all four points and check that all dimensions are correct.

When taking any measurements do not measure from the end of the ruler; always start 10mm from the end, remembering (as I confess I sometimes don't!) to **add** this on to the desired length. The ends of rulers become abraded and inaccurate; it is difficult to line up the end of a scale on a precise mark, but easier using the 10mm mark. If you have to mark a piece of plastic with numerous measurements (e.g. bolt holes), make these measurements cumulative rather than individual; any error will be isolated by this method, while individual measurements will compound any errors.

Materials

The most important material in scratch-building conversions is plastic, which is relatively cheap and the easiest material for the modeller to work. It can be bought not only in large flat sheets of various thickness but also in strips, rods and structural shapes. In England the sheet thickness is restricted to eight grades, which despite metrication 25 years ago are still expressed in imperial terms. The sizes in thousands of an inch (with nearest metric equivalent in parentheses) are 80 (2.0mm), 60 (1.5mm), 40 (1.0mm), 30 (0.75mm), 20 (0.5mm), 15 (0.4mm), 10 (0.25mm), and 5 (0.13mm). In addition to white plastic sheets, clear perspex is also available.

There are many sources for sheet plastic, but far fewer suppliers of strip, rod and special shapes. For strip and rod the main English manufacturer is *Slaters Plastikard*. Hollow rod is produced by *Sutcliffe Productions*, whose main customers are the model aircraft enthusiasts. *Plastruct & Evergreen Scale Models* from the United States produce an excellent and varied range of rod and strip; and recently an expanding range of structural shapes. While structural shapes have been available for some years the quality of these sections has been poor, leading me to use brass shapes in lieu of plastic. However, in 1995 Evergreen has begun to market a new range of high quality shapes which compare favourably with some brass products. I would describe the English producers as cheap, but the Evergreen range is quite expensive in this country.

Brass sections

Since learning to solder I have always been a great exponent of brass sections. I term these shapes "structural" only because they conform to structural steel shapes as found in the construction industry. In England *John Flack* is the only supplier who offers the complete selection of shapes and sizes, coupled with an outstanding by-return mail order service. Although an ideal medium to solder, brass section can be mixed and matched with any other modelling materials, its only limitations being the glues to attach it to those alternative materials. Careful consideration of these shapes, for example in the construction of a gun cradle, can allow later disassembly during the painting stage. Gluing an L-section to either side of the gun cradle and then a U-shape to either side of the barrel guides should ensure that the barrel will recoil. There are no special skills needed to obtain this movement other than precise measurement. When I scratch-build an open topped vehicle carrying a gun it invariably ends up working, with both vertical and horizontal movement together with recoil - purely to facilitate painting, of course, and not

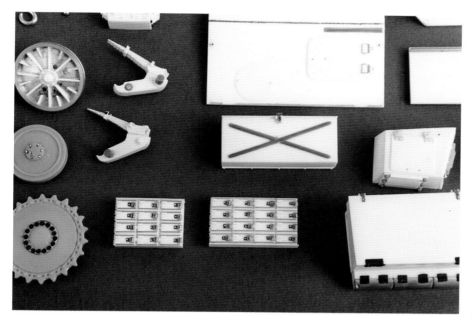

Joints

When two pieces of plastic are to be joined then you will need to decide on the joint. Many modellers always adopt bevelled joints (bevel: a surface that meets another at an angle other than a right angle) even for 90 degree joints; personally I always use butt joints on right angled joints. The only consideration is to deduct the respective plastic thicknesses from the overall external thickness. If you have raking 90 degree joints, then make a template of the required angle, or use a stainless steel protractor for setting or checking angles once the two surfaces are glued together. Use a plastic solvent for the initial set, leaving for a few minutes until the plastic cures. If the joint is to be exposed then apply the super-glue with fine wire to the internal face of the joint.

You can afford to be less immediately precise on the external joint. Generously apply both super-glue and baking powder to the complete external joint, finishing off with super-glue to seal the powder. The super glue/baking powder should be proud of the joint. Depending upon the extent of the filler, choose an appropriate file to remove the initial surplus. Use wetordry number P320 with water on one flat surface; then change to the other surface and repeat. You will observe that both the plastic and the filler will become matt as you sand. Between these two will be a small area of glossy untouched plastic. Change grades to P600 and continue. As you gently sand, this area of gloss will slowly decrease. Use your eyes and touch to judge when you have a perfectly clean joint. Not only will you have a clean, precise joint but the super-glue/baking powder will have added enormous strength.

With non-90 degree bends you will need to bevel the joints. Without the super-glue/baking powder you will need very precise bevels; with this method, near enough is good enough! Obviously, try for the best joint possible, but the excess filling method will mitigate any bad bevels. All surfaces should be wiped over finally with P1200 wetordry.

playing.... If the brass is to be attached to plastic then choose super-glue or epoxy depending on strength requirements. For soldering brass, see Chapter Six.

Basic construction principles

Main frames and components that are hidden from view should be constructed using the heaviest plasticard available. Once you have decided on the thickness of plasticard, remember to deduct this from the overall external dimensions. With the shape drawn on the plasticard and using your P-cutter and steel straight edge, scribe lines fractionally outside the required final edges. This will give you the minimum amount of cleaning up: it is easier to cut a line than to sand one. The P-cutter scribes a V-section in the plastic (this must also be allowed for). On thinner plastic card a single pass of the cutter should be sufficient; on 2.0mm plastic you may need

two or three. Under no circumstances cut through the plastic with the cutter; the most accurate method is to snap it. The edge of a table is ideal; with the scribed line on the exact edge of the table, support the remaining plastic with even pressure and apply firm downwards pressure. If necessary ensure even pressure by using the steel straight edge; smaller sections can be held with pliers and snapped. On the very thinnest plastic use your hobby knife to cut a groove similar to a plough with surplus plastic either side of the cut, which you will need to sand down after removal.

Once the plastic is cut or snapped it will need cleaning up. Use a medium grade wetordry paper. Do not sand in one direction only; however many movements you make in one direction, turn the plastic 180 degrees and repeat. The *True Sander* described in the tools chapter is especially designed to produce 90 degree or straight lines.

Left and above
Examples of the type of super-detail work which can be achieved with fine brass of various cross-sections, etched brass detail, lead foil, and plastic. These components were made up for the author's 15cm sIG 33 auf Fahrgestell PzKfw II.

Right
The completed 15cm sIG 33 (see also Chaper Nine).

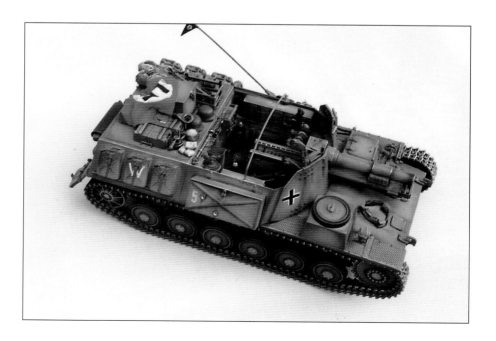

Below
The resin winch from the Bergepanther; this was the test shot from my plastic master. The main gearbox and large drum were made from laminations of plasticard; the wire cable is from nylon - this is preferred to cotton, which frequently has minute surface hairs which only become apparent during the dry-brushing process.

Bottom
Resin, plastic, white metal, copper and brass were all used in the modelling of this pulley and frame.

Lamination

If the item you wish to construct is over 2.0mm thick then you will need to laminate the plastic. If the component needs to be e.g. 8.5mm thick, I would choose four sections of No.80 (2.0mm) and one No.20 (0.5mm). From the template of the required shape cut out the five identical shapes and glue them together. Apply super-glue/baking powder to the exposed surfaces, and sand these to a clean, precise finish with wetordry. It is normally appropriate to make the template a little oversized to allow for gluing errors. Once again, remember never to sand excessively in one direction only - use the 180-90-180 degree technique.

To make circular objects I use the compass cutter to cut the plastic. Sometimes, however, the object is too small for the radius of the cutter, or the thickness required is in excess of the tool's capabilities. Your motor tool can also be used as a small lathe. If you need to reduce the diameter of the disc then drill a hole in the centre of the circle (the compass point is your marker) of the same size as your mandrel. Fix the disc to the mandrel, and at the slowest speed sand the disc down to the desired diameter. You can laminate discs in the same way as described above, allowing an extra 1mm over the required diameter before cutting from the card. Laminate the discs, drill through the centre, install the mandrel, and repeat the sanding technique. If the motor tool can be clamped then the side of a knife blade can also be used to reduce the diameter of the disc. Always finish off the disc with P1200 gauge wetordry.

This Panzerjäger was one of my first substantial conversions, using plastic, brass, copper and white metal. Very fine brass L-section rails are used on the gun cradle; U-section brass on the base of the barrel enables it to travel back and forth, making it easy to remove during the painting stage.

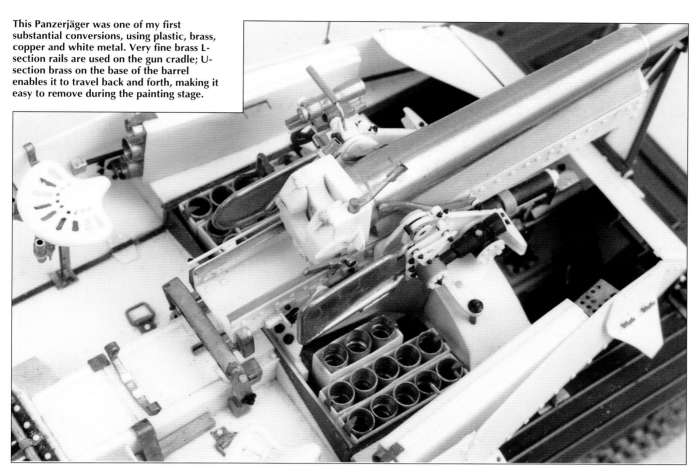

Even though this model would be described as a scratch-build, I consider it foolish to totally construct items such as e.g. the road wheels and tracks, when Model Kasten markets such outstanding products. There are very few models which are 100% scratch-built - they invariably incorporate some purchased accessories or spares.

CHAPTER SIX
SPECIALIST TECHNIQUES: ZIMMERIT, SOLDERING & VACU-FORMING

Any serious modeller of German World War II armour will at some point be confronted by the necessity to model **Zimmerit**. While the tank troops of many armies found themselves threatened by heroic infantry tank-killer squads armed with magnetic or adhesive charges, Germany was the only country to largely solve this problem by a technical innovation. Zimmerit was a special cementateous plaster-like substance which was factory-applied on all sloping and vertical surfaces of the tank; thickness varied but was generally approximately 12mm.

To further inhibit the magnetic or adhesive qualities of anti-tank charges the flat surface of the Zimmerit was broken up by patterning, which tended to follow fairly consistent lines. Most vehicles had a horizontal ridged pattern, although there were exceptions. The Panther's ridges were vertical with a scored square pattern over the ridge, while the Jadgpanther and some StuG/H IIIs had a small squared style; other StuG/Hs had either a ridge or a waffle pattern. In addition to vertical and sloping surfaces Zimmerit was also occasionally found on horizontal plates and side skirts.

Its use was almost exclusively restricted to tanks and StuGs produced from early 1943 to the autumn of 1944. Occasionally other vehicles (i.e. SdKfz 251 Ausf D) received a field-applied coat, but such exceptions are rarely found. As the emphasis of Germany's war changed from offensive to defensive strategy, so too did the use of Zimmerit decline; tanks lying in ambush do not tend to suffer attacks from infantry, and by the early autumn of 1944 its use was discontinued. (It is thus a useful contributory clue to dating the subjects of photographs.)

Obviously any modeller who produces a model tank from this period needs to be able to recreate this finish. There are two schools of thought about the most successful method. One follows the original method - application of a plaster material, and patterning with a purpose-made tool; the other recommends the use of a pyrogravure to burn the patterning directly into the surface of the plastic. Since my wife found the ideal tool for me to pattern the Zimmerit I have always used Milliput as a plaster substitute. There are occasions when I do resort to the pyrogravure, but these are infrequent and generally limited to Panzer IVs.

I have been totally satisfied with my results using Milliput, and although I keep an eye on the various alternatives as they come on the market I don't believe there is any way to date that I can improve upon the authenticity of the finish. The tool I use comes from a women's shoe-heel repair kit; it is used for spreading the glue, and has a perfect scale serrated ridge, measures 44mm x 14mm, and is therefore the perfect handling size. Modellers in England have been able to buy this gadget from Woolworth's; fortunately for

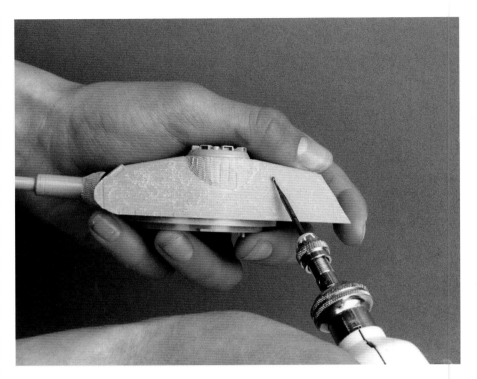

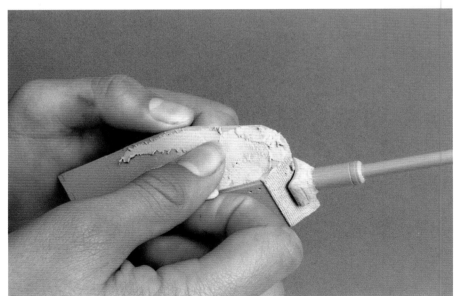

Top
Before applying Milliput for the Zimmerit, the surface of the plastic needs to be "scabbled" to provide the putty with a good key or grip; the process is similar to the rough-cast technique, and once again, the surface of the plastic should be cleaned up afterwards with steel wool to remove plastic swarf.

Above
With a hard drawing action, pull the freshy mixed Milliput towards you from the furthest point of the surface to be coated with Zimmerit.

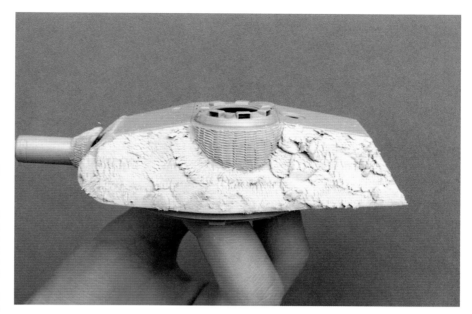

Right
The Königstiger turret completely covered with a rough coat of the filler.

Centre
With generous use of water and a plastic spatula, bring the Milliput to a smooth, approximately level finish.

Bottom
Again using copious quantities of water to prevent the Milliput lifting, start ridging furthest away from you. Complete only a few rows before cleaning the tool, re-wetting, and starting again.

those in other countries, Tamiya now produce an etched metal Zimmerit tool set with a number of optional shapes and sizes to cover all contingencies of restricted access. Other than the ridging implement, the only other tool required is a flexible plastic spatula to spread the Milliput.

Due to the slow curing of Milliput it is essential that only one or two surfaces are treated in each modelling session. Select the surfaces to work upon. To obtain better adhesion it is advisable to scabble (roughen) the surface of the material. This is easily achieved with a burr in a motor tool; roughen the surface and clean with steel wool - leave no residue of plastic swarf on the surface or this will contaminate the Milliput. Until you develop mastery of the technique, mask adjacent areas with tape. Mix only sufficient Milliput to cover the areas to be treated - but a little too much is better than having to re-mix near the end of the session. It is vital that the Milliput is fresh; if it shows signs of discoloration then buy fresh supplies. Old putty has a tendency to tear when applying the ridged effect. With a hard pressing action, and starting at the end of the surface furthest away from you, draw the Milliput towards you. When you have covered the whole area, dip the spatula in water and bring to a smooth and level finish. Use the edge of the spatula to remove surplus and uneven putty.

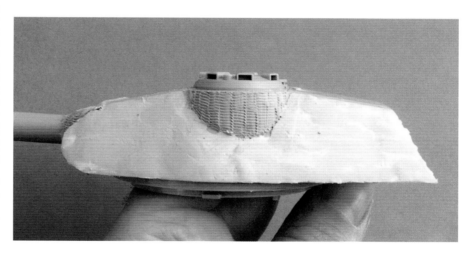

The next process is to apply the ridging with the tool. The implement I use has downwards facing serrations. This is most important, as when you apply a dark wash in the painting stage the residue lies in the recesses of the ridge, and thus, combined with dry-brushing of the pattern, provides depth and perspective to the Zimmerit. Copious quantities of water are required for the actual ridging process. Have paper towels or an old cloth handy. Wet the area you will immediately work on with your finger dipped into water. Dip the ridging tool also in the water and, once again starting furthest from you, commence ridging. Complete one row, 3mm-4mm wide, then commence a new row. Once you have completed four or five rows clean the ridging tool of all surplus Milliput. Dampen the next area, and repeat until a complete side is finished. With a pin or the end of a hobby blade lift any masking selotape you may have used. You will be surprised how easily this technique produces a neat, clean line. Scoring, i.e. for Panthers and StuG/Hs should be done after approximately one and a half hours, after which time the Milliput will have started to cure and will tolerate careful handling. Use a set square and hobby knife to score the squared pattern; try to avoid resting

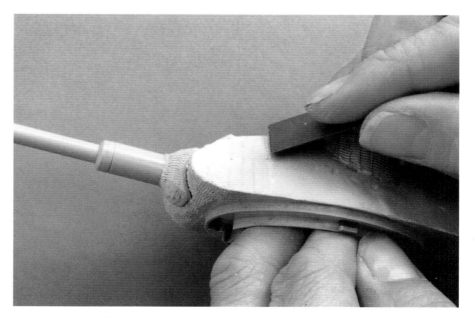

the set square on the Milliput.

If you have detail parts which need to be attached to the model within an area of Zimmerit you can adopt one of two methods. For large areas, position the detail, draw around the periphery with a pencil, and apply Selotape over the area. With your hobby knife score along the pencil lines, and remove surplus tape. In one corner apply a another small, thin strip of tape, and reinforce the seal with super-glue. The tape should now only cover the location of the future detail. Milliput across the entire area; and immediately after completing the ridging process, lift the tape from the corner where you applied the strip - it may need encouraging with a hobby knife or pin.

When faced with attaching small details, I normally impress them into the wet Milliput. The exact position for attachment can be established by drilling through the plastic. Once the Zimmerit is applied I push a fine wire through the Milliput from the inside to locate the position exactly. If the surface of the Milliput is dry to the touch when you impress the detail, then apply water with a paint brush to the area of detail and the Milliput, thus ensuring a good adhesive joint. If the impressed detail is in contact with the original plastic then plastic glue will give further strength.

Although the Milliput adheres superbly, battle damage can be authentically reproduced by penetrating its surface to the plastic underneath and then flicking small sections off. You have recreated Zimmerit in an identical manner to the original, and therefore it will behave in the same way as the

Top
The completed turret. When applying Zimmerit, restrict work to one or two different surfaces only per modelling session.

Above
Use either Selotape or insulating tape to mask detail not requiring Zimmerit while you work.

Right top
The PzKfw V Panther's characteristic vertically ridged Zimmerit applied in a "squared" scored pattern. Note also the scratch-built gun barrel clamp.

Right
The pyrogravure technique is time-consuming and demands unremitting concentration for a consistent effect - it is also all too easy to burn right through the plastic in a moment's inattention - but on the smaller vehicles like this PzKfw IV you have little alternative for Zimmeriting slightly sloping or horizontal surfaces.

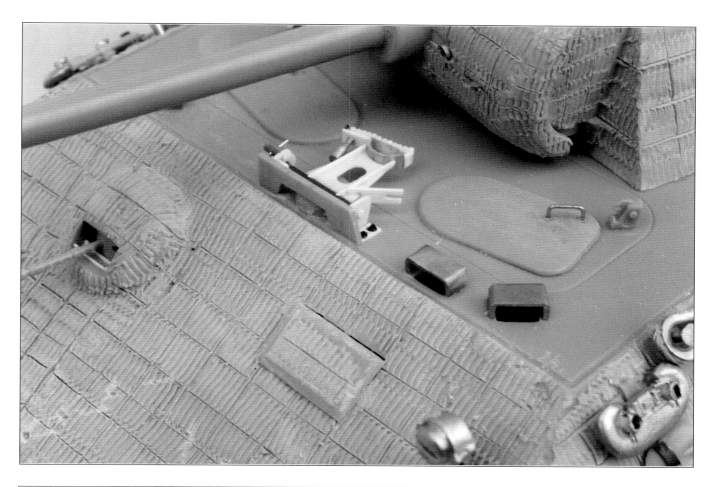

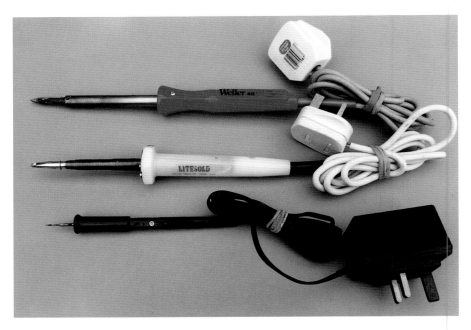

real Zimmerit. You cannot produce a more authentic coating.

Certain of the smaller vehicles - e.g. the Pzkfw IV - were also treated with Zimmerit, which in that case was additionally applied to some of its horizontal surfaces. Applying Milliput to such a small vehicle with such a lot of surface detail would obscure much of the latter. The only alternative is to use the pyrogravure technique, which is still popular with modellers who don't like the mess of the Milliput method. The pyrogravure I use was bought from Historex Agents for about £25.00. Its original use, with its long needle, was to detail the plastic Napoleonic figures from Historex, but it is quite a versatile tool - I use it not only for Zimmeriting but also for low melt soldering. The original point was too sharp and I have deliberately reduced the needle-like end to a blunter point.

Pencil the rows of the plastering pattern onto the plastic (3mm-4mm apart); and, with the point of the pyrogravure at a downwards slant, begin melting grooves into the plastic. If the tool is too hot, or applied with too heavy a hand, you can burn holes right through; use it too cool, and the plastic will string. I strongly recommend that you try the technique on a waste piece of plastic before starting on your model. Compared with the Milliput technique this is a slow and tortuous procedure, but unavoidable on some vehicles.

The waffle pattern as found on some StuG/H assault guns presents a real challenge. You will need to make up a special press mould. The only time I attempted this technique I was reasonably content with the result. I made a small square block of Milliput (4mm x 4mm). Once it had cured I cut vertical and horizontal lines into the surface, and attached a nail to the back of the block as a handle. Milliput was applied to the StuG in the manner previously described; then I impressed the surface of the block into the Milliput coating, watering and cleaning at regular intervals.

Soldering

Soldering is the technique of joining two metal objects together by fusing a limited amount of a third molten metal to both. This molten metal is relatively softer and melts at a much lower temperature than the metals to be joined; it is usually tin, although some of the specialist low melt solders are composed of entirely different minerals. In modelling AFVs the most common metals to be soldered are brass and copper, which are highly sympathetic to the technique. It is possible to solder certain other metals, such as aluminium and nickel silver, but these require not only specialist solder but the appropriate flux.

Why do we need to solder - would superglue or epoxy not serve as a substitute? The

answer is a highly qualified "yes"; but the attraction of soldering is that it provides a clean and very strong joint. In circumstances where the components need to withstand stress or weight then the correct solution is to solder the joints. Soldering has no hidden mystery and is almost entirely a matter of simple techniques accessible to anybody who uses a paintbrush. As with any facet of modelling, ease of handling is the secret of success: if you cannot hold or temporarily support the components in a satisfactory manner then you are almost guaranteed to have difficulty. Give careful consideration to the temporary support of the detail to be soldered (see Figs.3 & 45).

In addition to the usual hazards of modelling, soldering does involve the use of equipment which can operate at very high temperatures. Carelessness can lead to serious burns, and damage to furniture and surroundings; don't lose concentration.

The following list includes the main tools required for all permutations of soldering. I use up to four different methods of heat application. For standard soldering I use a 40 watt soldering iron; the most common soldering irons operate at about 25 watts, but I believe the additional power to be beneficial - the quicker the heat is transferred to the metal, the less chance there is of temporary supports becoming displaced. I also have an expensive low melt soldering iron, which cost nearly £40.00 even eight years ago when I bought it from *Carrs Modelling Products*, a company specialising in soldering materials. It has a variable control to adjust the heat so that even the lowest temperatures can be obtained. Specially designed to work with white metal kits, this iron is a useful but not essential item. Modellers who have a pyrogravure for the application of Zimmerit will also be able to use it for low melt soldering. The last heat source is a small propane gas torch. Occasionally used for the larger soldering jobs or for heat-annealing metal, this should be handled with extreme caution, as it produces very high temperatures - in excess of 1000 degrees C. You can also make your own temperature adjusting iron by

incorporating a dimmer switch and light bulb in the electrical circuit; the brighter the light, the less current flowing to the soldering iron, and the lower the heat.

The modeller will need a variety of fluxes and solders. The purpose of the flux is to clean and prepare the metal surface. If you are going to solder a variety of metals it is essential that you have not only the correct solder for the job but also the compatible flux. Carrs retail at least seven different fluxes and six solders - each solder has a compatible flux. For difficult joints that also need a high temperature solder Carrs also sell a solder paint. If you were soldering, e.g., telescopic brass tubing and wished to avoid any visible joint, you could paint the internal surfaces of the tubing with solder paint, and apply the heat; the liquid will turn to solid solder. I invariably use separate solder and flux; those solders that come with cored flux do not give clean joints, and I avoid them. In order to position components together temporarily I normally use double sided or insulating tapes and/or the ubiquitous Blue-tac.

More than ten years ago in a model railway shop I discovered the delight of minute brass sections. The variety of size and section astonished me, and to this day I have continued to build up a considerable stock of these beautiful components. These sections follow all structural shapes, e.g. I, U, T, L and

Z-beams, together with hollow and solid square, rectangular and circular sections, and can be bought in a wide variety of sizes. While most model shops do not stock the range of sections, they do provide flat brass or copper sheeting of various thicknesses. Automotive suppliers are a good source of brass shims as used in the installation of cabs on trucks, etc. For a few pounds you can buy sheets of brass, in up to five different gauges, which can be cut up into the required shapes and sizes.

One of the most difficult soldering tasks is to join more than two metals together. Multiple soldering can be frustrating, and its success is dependent upon good temporary supports and careful planning of different soldering tasks. For the initial solder you should chose the very hottest solder; Carr's No.243 is ideal. After the initial solder has set, lower melt solders should be adopted. You will need to adjust the heat of the iron down so that your previous work will not re-melt.

Before you even start soldering you should clean and prepare the respective surfaces; unclean components mean poor adhesion and erratic, uneven solder. I normally clean brass sections and sheet metals will steel wool. Before removing any item of etched brass from the fret it should be cleaned. Be very careful if you use steel wool; it is extremely easy to buckle and bend fine detail on the fret, and not so easy to straighten out. The glass fibre cleaning pens are also very helpful; dip the end of the pen in washing liquid and clean the brass, before rinsing thoroughly in clean water and drying.

If the parts being soldered are not etched but brass sections then do not cut them to size; do this after you have soldered. It is much easier to hold in position a piece of brass section 100mm long then a piece which may only be a couple of millimetres. If the joint is acceptable then it will have sufficient strength to withstand the stress of cutting with a slitting disc in your drill. If you should be soldering etched metal details, then do not remove all sections at once - leave the largest component on the fret. It is easy to attach the whole fret to your work top. The smaller etched parts can be soldered to the main part, and this can be removed from the fret after completion.

The tip of the soldering iron should be clean and covered only with a thin film of solder. If the end is black then it needs cleaning; this should be done with a file, and once the copper is exposed it is ready to be re-tinned. Solder should come directly from the soldering iron, not independently from the solder stick. Heat the iron until it will sizzle when immersed in the flux. When this occurs touch the end of the iron with the solder. The solder should jump to the iron. The surface of the tip should not hold excessive solder; if it does, give a hard flick to shake the excess off. You will need a temporary support for the iron while you are not immediately using it; I also keep handy a small wet sponge to wipe the excess build-up of contaminates off the tip.

When you are completely prepared, you will need to apply a small amount of solder to each of the respective components. You will not be applying solder to the joint - merely heat. Once the heat is applied to the joint, solder on the two surfaces will melt, fuse, and

re-solidify once the heat is removed. I tend to use pliers to hold even small objects; tweezers have an uncomfortable habit of springing the object into space! Holding the item, dip the section that is to receive the solder into the flux paste; if you have liquid flux, then apply it with a paintbrush. Tin the iron; ensure that there is no excess solder; then touch the object with the iron. Solder should flow to object. Tin all components. Prepare the positions of the objects; the tape or Blue-tac used to fix temporary supports are affected by heat, but if your preparation is correct the heat will be limited to only a few seconds. If you are to add to existing soldered joints then you will need to reduce the heat of the iron, and change both flux and solder. Repeat until completion. Do not worry too much about excessive solder; this is best cleaned up after the operation is complete.

With brass sections you may well need to not only cut, but also shape with a powered tool; I use the slitting discs for both tasks. With a little practice complicated shapes can be made by use of these discs. They are also a

lot safer for cutting joints than a manual saw. Use the drill on a medium speed - not too slow, or the cutting edge can bite and stick in the brass; and not too fast, or you lose ability to control the work. The green silicon carbide discs are the perfect tool for cleaning the

Below
Here I am working with brass rod, previously heated with a propane torch and then quenched in water to anneal or soften it. Both the brass sections to be soldered have been tinned and are held in place by Blue-tac. The iron merely produces the heat for the two separate applications of solder to fuse together.

Bottom
Additional elements are soldered on. Heat is only applied for long enough for the two sections to fuse - any longer, and you risk remelting previously completed joints. Observe the build-up and deterioration of the soldering iron tip; it will soon need filing down and re-tinning.

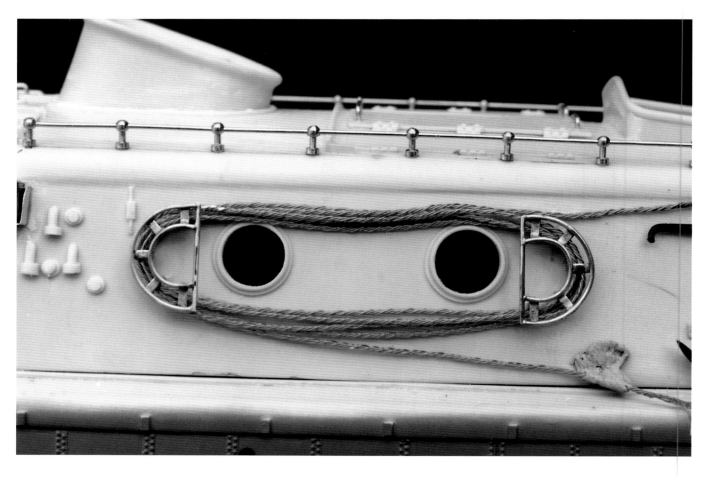

Above
The finished job - neat cable reels, glued into position on Mini Art Studio's Landwasser model.

joints; when new they have an excellent edge which will remove any excess solder from a joint. Be careful not to remove too much solder, however: after all, it is the basis of the strength of the joint. Once complete the joint should be washed with the glass fibre pen and

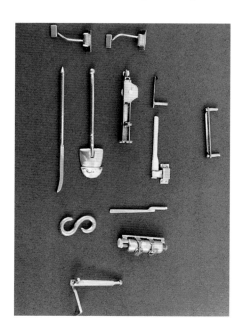

washing liquid, and thoroughly rinsed.

The soldering of white metal requires no additional techniques. You have a choice of iron: either the purpose made adjustable type, a pyrogravure, or your own adapted standard iron. The first essential is to clean the white metal; a brass wire suede brush is ideal. The quality of white metal varies from manufacturer to manufacturer, and the melting point will depend upon the proportions of the base metals in the casting. Find a piece of the casting sprue to test before starting to soldering; if the soldering iron melts the white metal then adjust the temperature control down until it has no effect.

Carr's No.70 solder and Red Label flux work extremely well on most white metals. The solder operates at such a low temperature that handling is even possible. The joints produced by these low melt solders are considerably weaker then hotter solders, and therefore should be treated with greater caution; but they are still stronger than most glues. The pyrogravure is the ideal tool to solder white metal tracks, as the fine pointed end enables the modeller to reach areas not accessible to the standard chisel end of a conventional soldering iron.

The serious modeller should not hesitate to learn and master the discipline of soldering; it enables you to work with finely detailed etched brass and sections, and adds strength and finesse to your work.

Vacuum- and heat-forming of styrene

About ten years ago the "cottage industry" produced quite a range of vacuum-formed kits, which gave the small specialist firms the chance to produce economically a variety of subjects not covered by the major manufacturers. The introduction and perfection of resin kits has largely led to the demise of this technique. The ability to produce large, perfectly matching sectional parts with fine detail was very limited, and vacuum-formed kits often caused modellers a good deal of frustration.

However, the forming of styrene shapes by either vacuum or simply the application of heat and pressure does offer the modeller the ability to make small, complex, thin or difficult shapes to a high standard. There are, for example, many occasions when items need to have a strengthening rim added to them - gun shields and cradles, seats, etc. The technique also enables the construction of objects with compound curves, since in theory literally any shape can be formed.

Left
Brass tools, which I always solder together for greater strength.

Right
This anti-aircraft machine gun mount for a Bergepanther called for the use of a number of solders with different melting points. The threat of all the joints suddenly dissolving during the last part of the operation was a nightmare which I finally overcame.

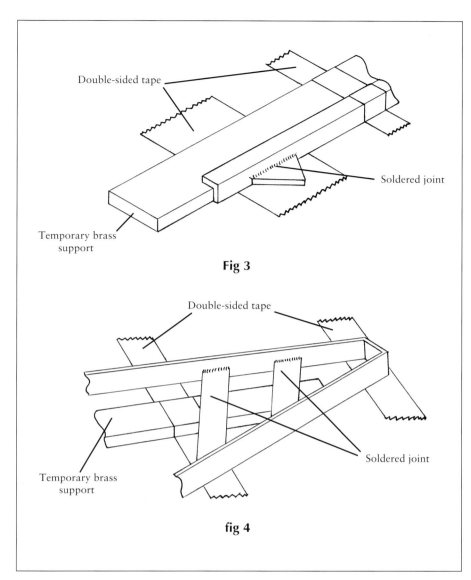

Double-sided tape

Soldered joint

Temporary brass
support

Fig 3

Double-sided tape

Soldered joint

Temporary brass
support

fig 4

Figs.3 & 4: the temporary supporting of components during soldering, as described in the text.

Styrene, a thermoplastic which is normally hard, becomes soft and flexible when gentle heat is applied. Once the heat source is removed the plastic rapidly cools and hardens, retaining the new shape. Vacuum-forming involves applying a sheet of hot, softened plastic over a pattern, and subjecting it to suction, which pulls the styrene down over the pattern to form the required shape. Without a vacuum the same technique can be attempted simply by physically forcing the hot plastic over the mould shape; but this method is far cruder than vacuum-forming, and you may need to repeat the operation several times before you achieve the desired finish.

The British reader is at a disadvantage here, as no maker in this country sells a vacuum-forming machine for modellers. I have a small American machine which has had its electrical supply altered from DC to AC and the voltage adjusted. To any reader of American modelling magazines, the number and variety of machines is staggering. It is fairly simple to build your own machine, and I would especially recommend articles on the subject in *Fine Scale Modeller* magazine dated October 1986 and January 1990. I will only describe here the simple technique of pulling a shape over a pattern. If you purchase a new machine then sufficient instructions come with them; and if you make your own from these articles, they adequately cover the method of operation. The following method is simple

Below
The Panzerjäger's basket looks like an appalling task, but was in fact fairly easy. Notches were cut in the main frame and the fine rod taped into position first; on this occasion solder was applied to the joint - no prior tinning was used, as this would have blocked the notches.

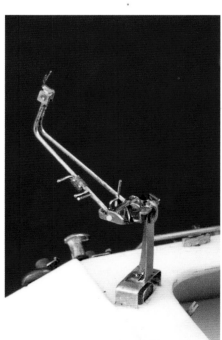

and effective; but bear in mind that it will not, repeat not, produce undercuts.

The only component that needs constructing is a frame to hold the plastic safely while it is being softened over a heat source. Two sheets of 6mm thick plywood are ideal. The basic rectangular shape should be approximately 225mm x 150mm; from this you need to cut out the centre to give a frame size of approximately 150mm x 100mm. This should leave you a safe working edge to hold, approximately 40mm wide both sides. Temporarily fix the ply sheets together and drill 5mm holes around the periphery of the frame - six should be enough - to take short nuts and bolts to clamp the two halves together. Lay your plasticard sheet over one of the frames; cut it to size, and with a hobby knife cut out the bolt holes. Position the top ply frame and insert the nuts and bolts, thus holding the plastic firmly in place.

The master pattern should be of sufficient depth and strength to withstand the downward pressure applied to it without distorting the shape. The pattern needs to be held on a vertical shaft so that the soft plastic can be pulled down over the shape; I normally insert a brass rod about 150mm long into the master pattern, and clamp the rod in a vice. An important consideration before making the master pattern is to decide on the thickness of plastic card to be used; an ideal thickness for all forming is 0.4mm (15/1000). Your master pattern must therefore take account of this thickness, or the formed plastic component will be larger in size by this thickness.

For heating the plastic an indirect source is best; an electric cooker ring is ideal. Gas should be treated with great caution. If you have no alternative then use the gas at its lowest setting. Oven gloves may be needed if your frame is small. The frame should be held approximately 150mm above the heat source. You will observe that as the plastic heats up it rapidly expands and starts to sag in the middle. Do not allow the plastic to sag too much; as soon as you are confident the plastic is sufficiently pliable, remove it and pull it down over the pattern. Do not use excessive force, or you will only tear the plastic and have to start again. Remove the plastic from the frame and cut the shape out. Use standard modelling techniques to clean and prepare the plastic.

The one great advantage with the vacuum technique is that the plastic is also drawn under the master pattern, producing undercuts and sharper corners and edges. If you have gone to the trouble of making the frame, then making the whole machine is only another evening's work away. One final reminder: the gases given off by plastic once ignited are highly toxic - be careful not to inhale them.

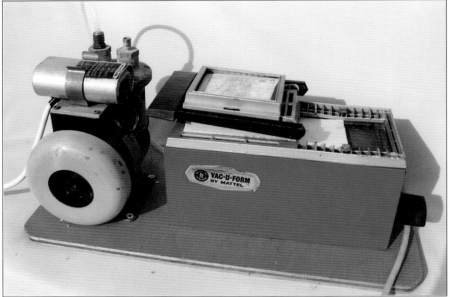

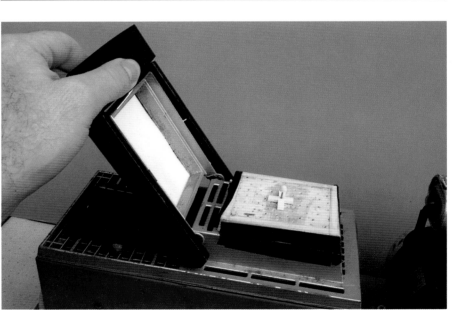

Above left
My converted vacuum-forming machine. A friend added a small electric pump after the original manual pump failed.

Above
The shape to be formed, in this case a headlight. The cruciform base is to stop the master falling over. The master was made in the drill from a piece of resin.

Left
The plastic sheet ,left, has been softened by heating over an element. It is about to be placed over the male mould, and a vacuum will be formed by the air being sucked out through the holes by the pump.

Left
The plastic sheet after the vacuum pump has pulled it snugly down over the male mould.

Far left
The master, and the newly formed headlight carefully cut from the plastic sheet.

Left
An MV Products lens installed inside the hollow headlight; it has taken quite a lot of work - but compare its appearance with that of the headlight (right) provided with the resin kit.

Below
The Panzerjäger's seat was also vacuum-formed (the holes, however, were cut afterwards).

CHAPTER SEVEN
PAINTING, WEATHERING & FINISHING

Of all the chapters in this book, this is by far the most important. It is upon the appearance of the finished model that your ability will be judged. While mistakes in construction can be masked, problems and errors at the painting and finishing stage will always be there to silently rebuke you.

Painting, like most of the other facets of modelling, is largely a matter of practice and technique. There is, however, some inherent skill in understanding what paint scheme will look best on any given vehicle. This cannot be taught; you must try to use your own imagination.

I am frequently criticised for my finish, which some describe as "too pretty". I make no excuse for this; I model first and foremost for my own pleasure, and my collection is planned to represent the vehicles used by the German Wehrmacht - not the mud and dust they fought in! My collection is technical and representative of these vehicles. Were I to build dioramas then the finish would need to be in sympathy with the ground. However, I can't help feeling that some of those modellers who cover their vehicles liberally with mud choose this approach to mask their inability to paint their models to a reasonable appearance. All models need a degree of weathering, of course, unless they specifically represent vehicles straight out of the factory; it is the degree of weathering that demands judgement. I, too, have used the application of mud to hide construction errors, be they mine or the manufacturer's; but I would never accept excessive use of mud as a means to complete one of my models.

This chapter falls into three sections: brief comments on German AFV camouflage and insignia; the materials and equipment needed to reproduce these; and their application.

CAMOUFLAGE, MARKINGS & INSIGNIA

There is no space here to delve too deeply into this subject, which is a science in its own right. I would highly recommend the three volumes entitled *Panzer Colours* by Bruce Culver and Bill Murphy (see Appendix). The first volume covers the camouflage of the German Panzer forces, the second the markings, and the third the specialised units, Waffen-SS, and Luftwaffe. I could not describe any of these volumes as being the definitive work on the subject - e.g. the *Niehorster* series on organisation will finally run to thirteen volumes, in contrast to a single chapter in *Panzer Colours 2*; but these three books provide an excellent grounding in this complicated subject.

Understanding the correct colours, divisional insignia and tactical markings is essential to achieving a historically correct model. The reader must also understand that certain vehicles were only assigned to particular units, and that these units only fought in particular theatres of operations. The importance of developing an interest in the preparatory detective work among pictorial and written sources cannot be emphasised too strongly.

I frequently give the following as an example of everything that can be historically wrong with a model even if the quality of the construction and painting is outstanding. Our model is a Tiger II "Königstiger" Ausf B with a Henschel turret, painted in three-colour ambush scheme, with Leibstandarte-SS Adolf Hitler divisional insignia, DAK Afrika palm, and turret numbers "899". What's wrong? Well, basically everything! The war in North Africa finished a year before Tiger Bs were introduced. The three-colour scheme was only introduced in early 1943 and supplies never reached North Africa. No SS units ever fought in this theatre. Most Tiger battalions had only three companies, the turret numbers therefore starting with the digits one, two or three. The second digit identified the platoon (Zug), and the third the tank within the platoon. Most battalions had up to 45 tanks with headquarters tanks additional; thus, turret numbers showed a great preponderance of the digits one to five. More than 45-50 vehicles in a Tiger battalion were very rare; so a Tiger with the numerals 899 is virtually impossible.

This is of course a deliberately extreme example, to underline the fact that the modeller has to consider many different factors before he picks up a paintbrush. Do not rely solely on the suggested scheme illustrated or described in the kit instructions; these often contain many mistakes. As a minimum, I would recommend careful preliminary study of the Bruce Culver series.

The German system of vehicle camouflage was the most highly developed among all the combatant armies. The final war colour scheme of three colours continues to influence contemporary military forces. Although the vehicles were issued from the factories in a basic paint finish the crews were issued with

Left
A drawer full of paints, enamels on the left and acrylics on the right. This is arguably an excessive stock, but most modellers nurse a well-founded fear that favourite materials may suddenly become unavailable - Compucolour is a prime example of an excellent paint that was discontinued.

concentrated paint paste for field application of camouflage. Most tanks were equipped with compressors, so sprayed finishes were possible. Equally, the paint could be brushed on; and application of paint (or whitewash) was not restricted to brushes or sprays - mops, rags, brooms, and even hands were sometimes employed. Depending upon the degree of dilution of the paint and its method of application, we find endless permutations of colours and schemes. This variety is one of the prime reasons for my interest in German vehicles.

Wartime paint colours

Even 50 years after the end of the war there is still some controversy over the interpretation of German colour shades. The *Panzer Colours* series (in particular the first volume) describes in considerable detail the Heeres Memorandum (HM) relating to specified colour changes to be adopted by Army vehicles. While I have no disagreement with the dates and memorandum numbers, I cannot always agree with the colour descriptions associated with these orders or with those included in the text.

Only after photographing part of my collection with black-and-white film did I fully appreciate the tentative nature of the conjectures found in most written sources on this subject - from my own photographs it was impossible to be precise over whether a colour was basically Olivgrün or Braune, let alone to identify some of the subtler shades. Dilution of paint, photographic light conditions, quality of film and temperature all had an effect on the production of the print. Every modeller who takes photographs of his work will know that even with today's rigorous quality control of film and processing there can be substantial differences in tone. Statements based on interpretation of wartime monochrome photographs should therefore be treated with great caution, and it is not surprising that contradictory opinions will often be found. (A single example comes from two books copyrighted by the same company: on page 87 of *Panzer Colours 3* we have a

Tiger I of sSS-PzAbt 101 with a turret number described as "red and white"; on page 3 of Squadron Signal's *Tiger in Action* the same photograph is captioned as "light blue with yellow outlines").

The final ingredient in this conundrum is the paint itself. Almost all hobby paint manufacturers have at some stage produced ranges purporting to be wartime German ground forces colours; but I would suggest that most are inaccurate. In May 1991 my colleague Heiner Duske wrote to the RAL Deutsches Institut für Gutesicherung und Kennzeichnung e.V. (loosely, "German Institute of Quality Control & Identification"). Funded by the chemical industry since 1925, this is the equivalent of either the British Standards or the US Federal Color Standards; and comments received from this organisation should therefore take precedence over all other sources. Herr Duske received not only comprehensive information on the chronological introduction and deletion of the Second World War colours, but also authentic paint chips. From these chips *Hannants* of England and *Gunze Sangyo* of Japan have produced a range of modeller's paints. Hannants enamels cover the full ten shades, while Gunze produce a more limited range but in lacquer. Below will be found a list of the RAL colour numbers, with descriptions where given, and the Hannants product reference code in brackets.

Regrettably, Dunkelgelb - arguably the most important colour - has no RAL number. The paint chip produced by RAL is sometimes described as "too dark" or "too olive"; but the reader should note that the German description of the colour is "dark yellow" - would lighter shades qualify for this description? On a visit to the Patton Museum in spring 1995 we were shown an SdKfz 251/9 Ausf D under restoration. After careful removal of the American overspray we were shown up to five distinct shades of Dunkelgelb on the one vehicle! The absence of a RAL reference is perhaps the clue to the lack of agreement over the correct shade. Without a definitive specification it is likely

that different wartime manufacturers produced variations of colour shade. I can only surmise that the RAL chip represents what Dunkelgelb *should* look like.

Finally, modellers should note that paint is produced as if you were painting a full size vehicle. Allowances for scale effect are the modeller's responsibility; remember that the smaller the scale, the lighter the shades of paint will need to be for a realistic appearance.

RAL 7021 Schwarzgrau (X800)
Used until February 1943; also in conjunction with RAL 8002.
RAL 7016 Anthrazitgrau (X802)
Used by Luftwaffe ground forces e.g. Hermann Göring Regiment.
RAL 7008 Khakibraun (X804)
Used by Afrikakorps and in Crete, 1941; no official RAL description of colour; used in conjunction with RAL 8000.
RAL 7027 (X809)
Used by Afrikakorps after 1941; no official RAL description of colour; used in conjunction with RAL 8020.
RAL 6003 Olivgrün (X806)
Used in conjunction with RAL 8017 and Dunkelgelb.
RAL 8002 Signalbraun (X801)
Used in conjunction with RAL 7021, especially pre-1939.
RAL 8000 Grünbraun (X803)
Used by Afrikakorps and in Crete, 1941; no official RAL description of colour; used in conjunction with RAL 7008.
RAL 8020 (X808)
Used by Afrikakorps after 1941; no official RAL description of colour; used in conjunction with RAL 7027.
Dunkelgelb (X805)
Used as standard base colour from February 1943; no official RAL number; used in conjunction with RAL 6003 & 8017.
RAL 8017 Braune (X807)
Used in conjunction with RAL 6003 and Dunkelgelb.

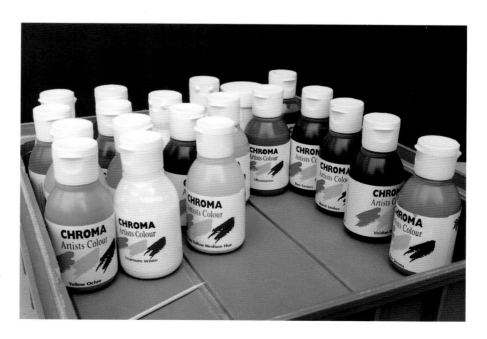

Right
The newest painting medium on the market, Chroma Artists Colour, is also the most versatile; water based, it will behave like any other medium, from water colour and acrylic to oil paints. There are up to 80 intermixable colours in the range, which is notable for very strong, vibrant pigmentation.

Vehicle markings:

German vehicles could potentially display a multitude of markings ranging from national insignia, vehicle numbers, tactical and divisional insignia, and victory tallies, to factory stencils indicating tyre pressures, vehicle weights, warnings - the permutations are endless. There is only space here to touch upon the main markings found on AFVs and reconnaissance vehicles; once again, the Bruce Culver books provide a good introduction to this extensive subject.

National insignia (Balkenkreuz)

During the war all armoured fighting, reconnaissance and personnel vehicles carried the "Greek cross" national insignia as an essential means of identification to friendly ground forces, and to the Luftwaffe with which they co-operated so closely in "Blitzkrieg" operations. For the attack on Poland in September 1939 the Panzer Divisions sported a white Balkenkreuz. After that campaign debriefings revealed that many vehicles had suffered hits due to Polish anti-tank gunners using the cross as an aiming point. Tank troops had already found this out, covering this prominent sign with mud to obscure its stark appearance. In autumn 1939 and for the operation against France and the Low Countries in spring 1940 vehicle crews painted either the whole cross in yellow, or its centre, leaving a narrow white border. From this temporary expedient developed the open cross, with a white border but with the centre left in the basic vehicle colour, then RAL 7021 (Schwarzgrau). Not until the campaign in North Africa in 1941 was it found necessary to fill in the centre of the cross in black; the white outline on a yellow/brown background was not visible at even medium ranges. Following the adoption of Dunkelgelb as the European theatre base colour in early 1943, so too did the black/white Balkenkreuz become standard.

The means of application also affected the size and appearance. Issued stencils provided the most professional appearance, and these were generally about 250mm square. Applications on Zimmerit were generally by hand and consequently varied in neatness.

Very few softskins manufactured in Germany or its satellites displayed the Balkenkreuz. However, all captured vehicles pressed into service by the Wehrmacht, including softskins, invariably displayed larger than normal crosses. In campaigns where the Luftwaffe enjoyed air superiority these crosses were frequently very large; the largest were, as one would expect, on the roof or top of these vehicles.

There were permutations on the standard Balkenkreuz throughout the war, but use of even the normal cross declined towards the end; and in the final months it was not unusual to find vehicles with no markings whatsoever.

Divisional insignia

In order to aid troops to identify their own units a system of visual identification was adopted. Up to the invasion of Russia in 1941 the system was rather erratic. Whatever system was to be adopted, it had to fulfill the dual function of being easy for Axis forces to

recognize, and confusing to the Allies. This ambiguous requirement saw the introduction of simple geometric designs, runic and other traditional symbols for the Polish campaign. With the dilution of the existing Panzer Divisions in order to double the number for the Russian campaign a more standardised approach was adopted. These new emblems for the eighteen Panzer Divisions were basically a series of permutations on runic symbols. However, for reasons of morale many divisions also displayed symbols more specific and traditional to particular units - e.g. the white oakleaf of the 1st Pz.Div., the Berlin bear of the 3rd, the "ghost" of the 11th, and so on.

As the war progressed the divisions of the Army and Waffen-SS were affected by many changing circumstances. Some Infantry, Cavalry, Panzer Grenadier and Fallschirmjäger formations were upgraded to Panzer Divisions, sometimes directly, sometimes by stages; and they too wished to retain their old emblems. However, despite the proliferation of traditional emblems the designated system of 1941 remained in use for much of the war. Up to 1941 these emblems were generally painted in a colour which would stand out from the base grey, white and yellow being the most common. After the introduction of Dunkelgelb the insignia tended to be painted in white, although those units with "non-regulation" insignia frequently used other colours such as black or red.

A basic guide to the better known of these insignia will be found in Fig.5 opposite.

Tactical numbering

Each German AFV had a radio, and a unique tactical number that enabled the unit commander to identify a particular vehicle and issue orders correspondingly. Again, there is space here only for a brief note on the basic numbering system.

Prior to the invasion of Russia in 1941 each Panzer Division had a complement of up to 400 tanks in two Panzer Regiments. Each regiment consisted of two battalions, and each battalion (Abteilung) had three or four companies. A company (Kompanie) had three or four platoons; and each platoon (Zug) had from three to five tanks. German tanks generally carried three digits applied to the turret; the first identified the company, the second the platoon and the third the position of the vehicle within the platoon. Command vehicles displayed a slightly modified system based upon prefixes; regimental staff vehicles carried numbers beginning with the letter "R"; 1st Battalion staff tanks were prefixed with the Roman numeral "I" and 2nd Bn. with "II". There were rarely more than three to five command vehicles for either regimental or battalion staffs, and therefore an allowance of up to two digits - e.g."R01", "II02" - was sufficient.

Preparations for the invasion of Russia saw a considerable expansion in the number of divisions, and a consequent dilution of the strength of the individual divisions. Neither vehicles nor crews were available to double the overall strength of the Panzer arm as instructed by Hitler, and most formations sacrificed one of their regiments to form the additional divisions. To compensate for this, most battalions thereafter fielded a minimum

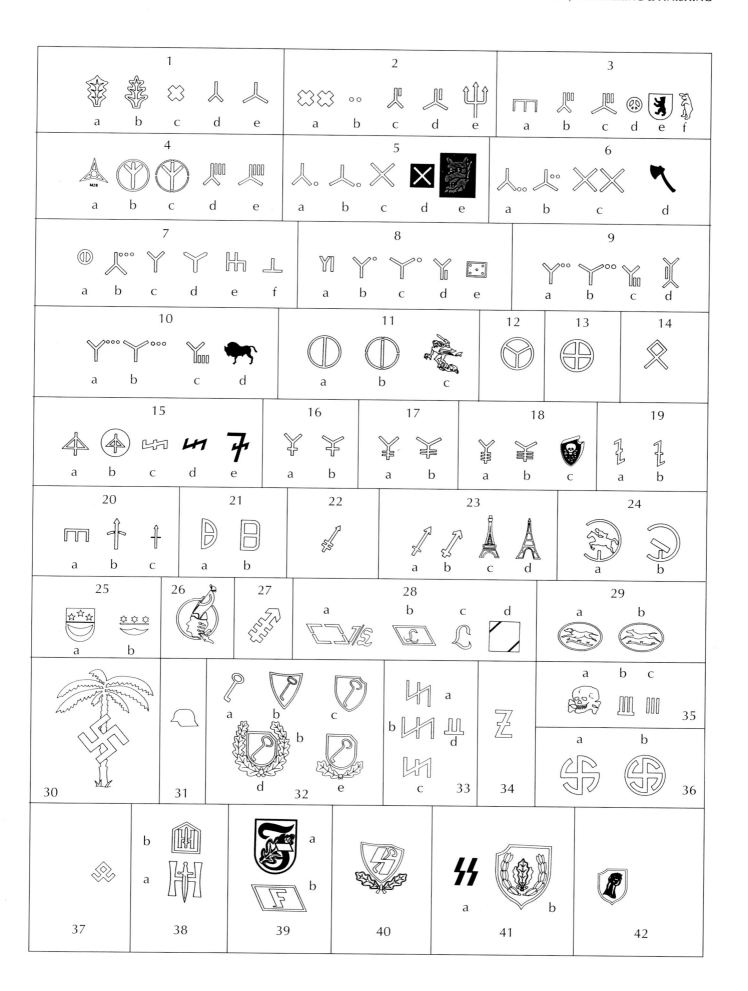

of four companies, with four platoons, and five vehicles per platoon (in theory - the realities of war meant that units were very seldom up to full strength).

This did mean an easing of the numbering system within the regiment. The four companies of the 1st Battalion were numbered 1 to 4, and those of the 2nd Battalion, 5 to 8. As newer equipment appeared it was further intended that the 1st Battalion was to be equipped with Panthers and the second with Panzer IVs.

Up to the invasion of France in 1940 most vehicles carried small rhomboid-shaped metal plates in Schwarzgrau (RAL 7021) with white numerals. However, in battle conditions these plates were difficult to see and therefore the practice of turret application became the norm. The battle for France was a transition period, with some numerals applied to the turret in white outline only, some with red in-fill, and some with the pre-war system. The white outline with red in-fill became the accepted practice for much of the war. Variations were observed, however, using all the primary colours; these are often hard to interpret with any confidence from black-and-white photographs. Towards the war's end the use of numerals declined, and in spring 1945 photographs show many vehicles devoid of markings. Numerals were generally applied by stencil; the use of textured Zimmerit precluded this, and many numbers were consequently hand-painted.

Almost all armoured fighting vehicles displayed these numerals, but their use on other vehicles was restricted. The reader should remember the tactical reason for numbering vehicles; therefore it was not unusual to find e.g. self-propelled artillery units without numbers. Armoured personnel carriers were used to carry troops into combat, and therefore most half-tracks sported tactical numbers. Originally intended to carry troops (SdKfz 251) or perform reconnaissance (SdKfz 250), these vehicles developed into a multitude of differing roles and variants, and almost all carried numerals. Early armoured cars used in the reconnaissance role were generally without tactical numbers; but as their uses multiplied so did the need for them to be individually identifiable, and thus we find many of the eight-wheeled vehicles with tactical numbers.

Tactical signs & tables of organisation

Virtually all German military vehicles carried symbols to identify the tactical unit to which they were attached. The symbols were based upon the official German handbook of military symbols issued on 24 March 1941 and entitled *Heeresdienst-vorschrift 272 (HDv 272)*, together with the actual symbols used in the organisational charts *(Kriegsgliederung des Feldheeres*, 15 May 1941). In January 1943 an amendment to HDv 272 was issued, updating the original instructions and bringing the tactical signs into line with alterations to equipment and organisation.

These tactical signs were generally applied to both front and rear of all vehicles, from tanks to lorries to motorbikes. Generally on the left hand side (facing forward), they were either stencilled or hand-painted in white. Used not in isolation but in a seemingly bewildering number of permutations, they provided the

experienced observer with a quick and exact method of unit identification. It is not possible to go into any detail on this subject, as it is the most extensive of all within the science of German vehicle markings; I can only recommend Leo Niehorster's excellent *"German World War II Organisational Series"*. I am very grateful to Dr. Niehorster for allowing me to reproduce examples of the organisational symbols, as Figs.6 & 7 in this chapter.

The foregoing paragraphs on the main markings found on German vehicles are by no means exhaustive; many vehicles also displayed other markings, including personalised names, tallies of combat victories, etc.; once again, the reader is referred to the printed sources listed in the Appendix.

MATERIALS

While most of my construction techniques and materials have tended to remain virtually unchanged, my approach to finishing my models has evolved, and continues to do so. As new paints arrive on the market I enjoy experimenting with these new mediums. It is not uncommon for me to use up to five different paint types on one model - though I tend to experiment on the periphery of the finishes, and the main finish and camouflage is always either enamel or acrylic.

Since my modelling time is finite, I want to spend all of my available hours on actually modelling - not on waiting for materials to cure or dry. By careful planning it is possible to avoid this dead time. For example, the choice of acrylics for the base colour means that enamel washes with thinners can be applied within an hour or two of the base acrylic colours, the change of mediums protecting the first stage from damage by the second. All the following materials are what I used in 1995; in time there will doubtless be additional alternatives on the market, and in time my chosen methods will evolve further.

Primers

Priming is essential to ensure that the paint will adhere to metal surfaces; it also gives a uniform base colour to your model so that finishing coats have an even appearance. I use an automotive acrylic metal primer applied from an aerosol can. Colour choice is not important, but it should not be a dark colour - I use either white or light grey. (If I use a particular technique for the subsequent dry print application of numerals, described later in this chapter, I would use the white primer.) The advantage of acrylic metal primer in an aerosol is that the spray is very fine, contracts on drying, and produces a smooth satin finish. It is very economical, and for about £3.00 - £4.00 up to ten models can be primed.

Paints

If I choose **enamels** for the base colours of a model then I only use *Hannants* range of authentic colours (see previous section on exact colour matches). These perform extremely well in an airbrush, but less well if hand-painting large areas by brush. These paints, formulated at my suggestion by Hannants, were made not matt but with a slight satin finish. The use of brushes seems to accentuate this, so that an uneven gloss finish

is often the result if large areas are applied by brush. For basic primary colours like black, white, etc., which I generally apply by brush, I use *Humbrol*. The only Humbrol colour I use through the airbrush is Matt Earth (No.29). The pigments used by Humbrol are in my opinion rather coarse, and do not perform very well in airbrushes. In my experience they also have a tendency to absorb subsequent coats of other colours without affecting the base colour; and varnish is also difficult to apply - despite many coats the base matt application seems impervious to change.

The factory matt finish of most real vehicles changes to satin after even a short time in the field, steadily burnished by daily contact, wear and tear. Completely matt vehicles at 1:35 scale are therefore inaccurate; more important, they have a lifeless appearance which is unattractive. This vital satin finish to the upper surface or superstructure should be contrasted with the totally matt lower hull or substructure. Mud, dust and rust are 100% matt, and Humbrol's Matt Earth is the ideal medium for this part of the finish.

Hannants also produce two essential metallic colours, Natural Steel (X502) and Oily Steel (X503), the latter being the most important. After many years I have finally found a satisfactory silver: Tamiya produce an enamel Chrome Silver paint marker, which I believe to give the best and brightest silver on the market, producing excellent results by dry-brushing techniques. One of the main problems of allegedly silver finishes is the size of the metal particles in the paint. If these are too large and become detached from the medium (varnish), then dry-brushing produces a dusting of metallic particles across your model - numerous, and difficult to remove. The particles in Tamiya's Chrome Silver are extremely fine, and when using it I have never experienced this problem.

The other paints which I frequently use are **acrylics**. The Tamiya range are of high quality and perform very well in an airbrush; indeed, I would recommend that the novice uses these paints when learning airbrush techniques. Tamiya acrylics are very user-friendly and far more sympathetic than enamels. As with Hannant's enamels they do not perform very well when hand-brushed over large areas. Acrylics dry very fast and cannot be properly reconstituted with a thinner once dry. They are excellent for painting detail.

A selection of **oil paints** are also essential to the armour modeller. It is very difficult to dry-brush with acrylics due to their rapid drying; and while enamels are more tolerant they are distinctly unfriendly to your sable brushes. Oil paints have a very long curing period (many days at room temperature); if used either in isolation or in conjunction with enamels they offer greater flexibility when dry-brushing. Oil paints are the ultimate choice for blending colours or painting ultra-fine detail. Other than the basic primary colours I have a preponderance of yellow and brown shades (some of these tubes are now more than 30 years old, yet still perform adequately if carefully stored). The most indispensable colour I use is Sepia Extra; this sooty brown/black is ideal for washes and recesses.

For painting numerals and some fine detail I use a new paint type which was designed for the cartoon film industry, called **Chroma artist's colours**. These paints are water based

Fig 6

GERMAN ORGANIZATIONAL SYMBOLS
1944 – 45

SIZE, FUNCTION, MOBILITY

General Headquarters	Army Group Headquarters	Army Headquarters	Group Headquarters	Corps Headquarters	Volks-Artillery Corps Headquarters	Military Commander	Division Headquarters	Brigade Headquarters	Volks-Artillery Brigade Headquarters	Regiment Headquarters	Battalion Headquarters
Infantry	Reconnaissance	Signal	Engineer	Bridging Engineer	Railroad Engineer	Technical	Supply	Motor Transport	Maintenance	Medical	Veterinary
Infantry	Mountain	Bicycle	Semi-Motorized	Motorized	Motorcycle	Armored Infantry	Panzer / Tank	Anti-Tank	Construction	Military Police	Cavalry
Artillery	Mountain Artillery	Self-Propelled Artillery	Panzer Div. Artillery	Artillery Observation *Bb*	Rocket Artillery	Recoilless Artillery	Assault Artillery	Infantry Anti-Aircraft	Army Anti-Aircraft	Luftwaffe Anti-Aircraft	Machine Gun
Foot / Horse-Drawn	Mountain	Ski or Sled	Bicycle	Mixed Mobility	Semi-Motorized	Motorized	Motorcycle	Halftrack Towed	Amphibious Motorized	Self-Propelled (Tracked)	Halftrack

WEAPONS

Weapon / Classification		Machine Gun	Anti-Tank Rifle	Infantry Gun	Mortar	Anti-Tank Gun	Rocket Launcher	Gun	Howitzer	Heavy Howitzer	Anti-Aircraft Gun	Flame Thrower
light	*le*	with bipod	to 79mm	to 75mm	to 79mm	to 39mm	to 109mm	to 99mm	to 129mm		to 36mm	man-packed
medium	*m*			80 – 119mm		40 – 59mm	110 – 159mm				37 – 59mm	
heavy	*s*	with tripod	over 80mm	over 76mm	over 120mm	60 – 89mm	160 – 219mm	100 – 209mm	130 – 209mm	210 – 249mm	60 – 159mm	vehicle-borne
super heavy	*sw*	over 15mm				over 90mm	over 220mm	over 210mm	over 210mm	over 250mm	over 160mm	

INFANTRY INSPECTORATE UNITS

Infantry Platoon	Infantry Company	Infantry Mortar Company	Infantry Machine Gun Company	Infantry Engineer Platoon *J*	Infantry Anti-Tank Platoon	Infantry Anti-Tank Company	Infantry Gun Platoon	Infantry Gun Company	Infantry Bicycle Platoon	Infantry Bicycle Company	Light Anti-Aircraft Co. (mot) *le*
Mountain Infantry Platoon	Mountain Infantry Company	Mountain Mortar Platoon	Mountain Machine Gun Company	Mountain Engineer Platoon	Mountain Anti-Tank Platoon	Mountain Anti-Tank Company		Mountain Infantry Gun Company	Mountain Bicycle Company	Lt. Mountain Transport Column *le*	Light Anti-Aircraft Co. (SP'd) *le*
Cavalry Platoon	Cavalry Company	Cavalry Mortar Platoon	Cavalry Machine Gun Company	Cavalry Engineer Platoon	Cavalry Anti-Tank Platoon	Cavalry Inf. Gun Platoon	Infantry Mounted Recon. Plt.	Light Infantry Company (motorized) *Jäger*	Machine Gun Company (motorized)	Mortar Company (motorized)	Medium Anti-Aircraft Co. (SP'd) *m*

ENGINEER INSPECTORATE UNITS

Engineer Platoon	Engineer Company	Mountain Engineer Company	Motorized Engineer Company	Armored Engineer Company	Engineer Goliath Company *G*	Engineer Assault Boat Company *Stubo*	Bridge Construction Company	Construction Company	Road Construction Company *Str*	Engineer Equipment Plt. (mot)	Railroad Engineer Company
Bridge Column *B* (motorized)	Bridge Column *K* (motorized)	Bridge Column *J* (motorized)	Unit of Bridge Equipment *H*	Unit of Bridge Equipment *leZ*	Unit of Bridge Equipment *sS*	Bridge Unit with Escort Detachment	Bridge Column Unit & Escort Detachment	Engineer Snow-Clearing Plt. (mot)	Light Engineer Transport Column (mot) *le.*	Engineer Park	Railroad Engineer Park

Right
Priming of models constructed from a mixture of materials is essential. Here a turret is being sprayed with a car acrylic metal primer. The spray is too indiscriminate to use indoors; wearing a glove is also recommended.

but mimic virtually every other painting medium, from watercolour, oils, acrylic, to gouache. They are probably the most versatile medium on the market. The pigments are also extremely strong, with a range of over 80 colours. Single coat application is generally sufficient; if I am hand-painting vehicle numerals, white on top of red still produces white, not pink as with so many other paints. Chroma artist's colours can also be used through an airbrush, though I have yet to experiment with them in this way.

Air recognition flags were an important means of identification for German vehicles up to 1943. My techniques require that both the paper and paint used are able to reconstitute themselves. For the paint I use **gouache**, which has strong and vibrant pigments. If the modeller has any problems with water based paints adhering to the model, then a tiny drop of washing liquid mixed with the paint will solve them.

Varnishes

The modeller has two options concerning the application of varnish: either during painting, or after. I adopt both methods, although my tendency is to add varnish to the basic colours as I spray, especially with acrylics. The problem with this technique is that different base colours do not always react in the same way when mixed with varnish, producing different intensities of satin finish. I use three different varnishes regularly: *Tamiya Clear (X-22)*, a high quality, durable gloss; *Hannant's XDSS semi-gloss Satin Varnish*; and *Rembrandt's Picture Varnish*. The last-named is thin and pure, and one light pass with the airbrush produces a beautiful light satin finish.

Thinners

All paints need a medium to transport the pigment; ultimately this medium evaporates - over hours, days or even months - leaving the pigment in its final position. To assist this movement - and to clean brushes and other applicators - we use thinners. For enamels and oils I use high quality white spirit; for acrylics, *Tamiya's X-20A thinner*. The other types of water based paint are thinned with clean tap water. I would add to this list one additional thinner, which should be treated with the greatest caution: this is cellulose thinners. This dangerous solvent is the ultimate for cleaning either hand- or airbrushes. A small addition of cellulose thinners to either acrylic or enamel paints will greatly assist flow characteristics, and will produce a slight etching of the paint to the surface. It must NOT be used without adequate ventilation.

Weathering chalks

I simply use artist's pastel chalks; so-called weathering chalks are in my opinion too greasy. Although I have a full colour range, I tend to use black, earth and orange to the

exclusion of most others. Most art supply shops carry the products of a variety of manufacturers; my own are German *Faber Castell chalks*.

Brushes

Buy the best that you can afford. It is undeniable that using enamels, acrylics and dry-brushing techniques is lethal to the life expectancy of your quality brushes. With the exception of a single hog hair bristle brush all mine are sable, which produces the best quality result but the emptiest pocket! For dry-brushing I use German *Premier* flat red sables, Nos.2 to 5; these are in my opinion the best on the market, giving commensurate results. While I have a variety of round brushes, from 00 to No.5, in practice I tend to use only the 00 to No.1. Most paint manufacturers also produce a range of quality sable brushes, and these can be very expensive. Due to my highly abrasive painting technique, for a good compromise between relative economy and quality I use *A.S.Handover* brushes. The application of weathering chalks is also very severe on brushes, and to dedicate a 00 or 0 round brush solely to this technique is sensible. I have a single pointed brush which is reserved exclusively for cleaning airbrush nozzles, etc.

Airbrushes & compressors

As mentioned above, most German AFVs were fitted with compressors, and therefore the majority of vehicles were airbrush-finished (though in the late war period certain "ambush" camouflage schemes were hand-brushed). The airbrush is therefore an essential tool to the modeller. Even if the camouflage scheme is to be brush-finished a good quality base colour can be applied in minutes with an airbrush, compared to the hours it takes with a hand brush; and it is very difficult to apply clean, regular, smooth applications of enamel or acrylic paint to large areas with a brush. The majority of the paints described above are specifically designed to work at optimum efficiency with an airbrush.

It would be inappropriate for me to recommend a particular manufacturer's airbrush and compressor, as my experience is limited to only one or two types. There are a substantial number of very good makes. Once you achieve satisfaction with a particular type you tend to stick to this brand, despite the availability of equally good alternatives. If you are buying an airbrush for the first time, break the golden rule for once - do not buy the best even if you can afford it! However, you should try to get a dual action brush. A single action brush is one that produces a constant thickness of paint line; by depressing the trigger a predetermined flow and thickness of paint is delivered to the surface. Dual action enables the operator to vary the thickness of the line during spraying by both downwards and backwards pressure on the trigger.

Why not buy the best if you can afford it? In addition to acquiring finesse of finger control on the trigger, you will also need to become a bit of a mechanical engineer. Disassembly, cleaning and reassembly of the airbrush can take longer than the actual painting of the model. Despite great care it is almost inevitable that you damage part of the mechanism either during spraying or when cleaning the fine needle. My main airbrushes are *DeVilbiss Super 63s*. The cost for a needle and head set (they are hand-made) is in excess of £60.00; and in one evening I managed through clumsiness to damage both head sets. Perhaps the reader can now understand my caution when recommending that the first airbrush purchased should not be the best. My Super 63 is regarded as the Rolls Royce of airbrushes, but as with a Rolls Royce the running costs can be prohibitive.

The majority of airbrushes need stripping down after spraying. Before purchasing any brush check with the shop or manufacturer the ease of stripping down and cleaning, as well as the quality of spraying. In the early 1990s *Kodak* produced the first radically different design of the traditional airbrush for more than 60 years. Originally titled the *Aztec*, this revolutionary brush offered all the advantages of traditional products but with superior ease of cleaning; the head assemblies were also priced very cheaply. Prices have

Fig 7

GERMAN ORGANIZATIONAL SYMBOLS
1944 – 45

PANZERTRUPPEN INSPECTORATE UNITS

Motorized Infantry Platoon	Motorized Infantry Company	Motorized Heavy Company (typical example)	Armored Infantry Platoon	Armored Infantry Company	Armored Flamethrower Platoon	Armored Gun Platoon

Armored Heavy Company (typical example) — Motorized Inf. Gun Company — Self-Propelled Inf. Gun Company

Motorcycle Recon. Platoon	Motorcycle Recon. Company	Kettenkrad Recon. Company	Motorized Recon. Company	Volkswagen Recon. Company	Armored Recon. Company	Light Armored Car Platoon

Heavy Armored Car Platoon — Armored Car Company (wheeled) — Armored Car Company (half-tracked) — Armored Car Company (tracked) — Light Recon. Transport Column

Tank Platoon	Tank Company	Radio-Controlled Tank Co.	Tank (Sturmgeschütz)	Assault Tank Company (Sturmpanzer)	Jagdpanzer Company	Armored Headquarters Company

Tank Maintenance Platoon — Tank Maintenance Company — Flame Tank Platoon — Motorized Anti-Tank Company — Self-Propelled Anti-Tank Company

ARTILLERY INSPECTORATE UNITS

Light Field Gun Battery	75mm Mtn. Gun Battery (GK 15)	75mm Cav. Gun Battery (FK 16nA)	Assault Gun Battery (Sturmgeschütz)	Independent Assault Gun Battery	Independent AG Battery (Alternate)	Light Field Howitzer Battery

105mm Field Howitzer Bty. (le. FH 16) — 105mm Field Howitzer Bty. (le. FH 18) — Heavy Field Howitzer Battery — 150mm Field Howitzer Bty. (s. lg. FH 13) — 150mm Field Howitzer Bty. (sFH 18)

Heavy Gun Battery	105mm Gun Battery (K 17)	105mm Gun Battery (K 18)	150mm Gun Battery (K 16)	150mm Gun Battery (K 18)	150mm Gun Battery (K 39)	150mm Gun Battery (How. Base)

170mm Gun Battery (How. Base) — 210mm Gun Battery (K 12) — 210mm Gun Battery (K 38) — 210mm Gun Battery (K 39) — 240mm Gun Battery (K 3)

240mm Howitzer Bty. (H 39)	210mm Howitzer Bty. (lange Mörser)	210mm Howitzer Bty. (M 18)	305mm Howitzer Battery	355mm Howitzer Bty. (M 1)	600mm Howitzer Bty. (Karl Gerät)	75mm Recoilless Bty. (LG 1)

105mm Recoilless Bty. (LG 2) — Army AA Searchlight Battery — 20mm Flak Army AA Battery — 37mm Flak Army AA Battery — 88mm Flak Army AA Battery

150mm Rocket Launcher Bty. (Nb. W. 41)	210mm Rocket Launcher Bty. (Nb. W. 42)	280/320mm RL Bty. (Nb. W. 41)	300mm Rocket Launcher Bty. (Nb. W. 42)	Sturmtiger Battery	Motorized Headquarters Battery	Hqs. Bty. Self-Propelled Battalion

Hqs. Bty. Assault Gun Battalion — Hqs. Bty. Army AA Battalion — Hqs. Bty. Rocket Battalion — Hqs. Bty. Art. Obs. Battalion — Artillery Park

Motorized Calibration Detachment	Mountain Calibration Detachment	Calibration Platoon	Calibration Battery	Weather Detachment	Motorized Weather Platoon	Sound-Ranging Battery

Flash-Ranging Battery — Motorized Balloon Platoon — Artillery Transport Column (mot) — Army AA Transport Column (mot) — Rocket Transport Column (mot)

SIGNAL INSPECTORATE UNITS

Motorized Propaganda Company	Motorized Signal Company	Motorized Telephone Company	Mountain Telephone Company	Telephone Construction Company	Wire Construction Company	Telephone Operations Company

Motorized Radio Company — Motorized Interception Company — Armored Signal Company — Armored Radio Company — Light Signal Transport Column (mot)

REAR ECHELON UNITS

Horse-Drawn Transport Column (15t)	Horse-Drawn Transport Column (30t)	Horse-Drawn Transport Column (60t)	Motorized Transport Column (30t)	Motorized Transport Column (60t)	Motorized Transport Company (90t)	Motorized Transport Company (120t)

Motorized Light Supply Company — Motorized Heavy Supply Company — Motorized P.O.L. Col. (25cbm) — Motorized P.O.L. Col. (50cbm) — Motorized Water Tanker Col. (60cbm)

Motorized Bakery Company	Motorized Butchery Company	Mot. Rations Administration Detachment	Motorized Field Post Detachment	Motorized Military Police Platoon	Motorized Military Police Company	Motorized Armorer Company

Field Hospital — Medical Company — Motorized Ambulance Platoon — Veterinary Company — Mot. Horse Transport Column

Motorcycle Messenger Platoon	Motorized Maintenance Platoon	Motorized Maintenance Company	Motorized Spare Parts Detachment	Motorized Spare Parts Column	Motorized Recovery Platoon	Tank Recovery Platoon

Motorized Mapping Detachment — Motorized Printing Detachment — Motorized Printing Platoon — Motorized Trains — Motorized Technical Company

fallen considerably since the first introduction, and they can now be bought for under £60.00.

The other essential is the compressor which services the brush with the necessary air; again, the modeller faces a huge choice. Prime considerations are the regulator for air pressure, moisture trap, reservoir and noise reducer. Your airbrush will need different air pressures - general spraying of large areas is best done at a higher pressure than fine detail work, so a variable pressure control valve is essential. You should also consider that Aztec type airbrushes work on a higher air pressure than standard products. Water vapour is found in air; when air is pressurised some of the water vapour condenses and forms tiny droplets, and unless these are trapped they will produce disastrous results when spraying. Your compressor will therefore require a moisture trap, fitted to the exit before the entry to the airbrush hose. For your own and your family's sanity I would strongly recommend a silenced version; the heavy rhythmic sound of an unsilenced compressor is a severe distraction. Lastly, the reservoir type is also to be recommended. Those compressors that do not have this facility rely exclusively on the airbrush hose to contain the

air, and a typical consequence is a pulsing type of paint finish. A reservoir stores the compressed air and releases it at the prescribed rate and constant pressure. A compressor with all these facilities is likely to cost in the region of £200.00 - £250.00.

The only alternatives to a compressor are either aerosol cans or a compressed air tank. The first alternative is horrifically expensive in the long run, and as the air pressure in the can decreases so too does the pressure reaching your airbrush. Substantial quantities of air are also required for cleaning the brush; if you run out of air before you can do this, you have a potential disaster on your hands. If you do have a pressurised container, as found for example in pubs to supply pressurised air to the beer pumps, then this may well be a feasible alternative. A garage should provide free compressed air to fill these tanks; but you will still need a moisture trap and regulator. If you can fill up with clean compressed carbon dioxide then the trap can be deleted (ensure a well ventilated room, to guard against oxygen depletion). I have used all these methods; but the only really satisfactory one is the compressor.

In addition to the painting materials and applicators you will also need the inevitable miscellaneous items. Perhaps the most important is an artist's mixing palette. The best are enamelled clay with up to six recesses. Masking film is also frequently used to achieve clean edges, e.g. for white air recognition bands. For masking windscreens, headlights, etc. during spraying I often also use *Humbrol's Maskol*, a rubberised solution

which solidifies once exposed to air and can be easily removed (provided it is within 24 hours) with a cocktail stick. A large supply of either clean lint-free cloth or kitchen towels is essential for cleaning up. Small glass containers for holding thinners and solvents are useful, together with a pipette or eye drop dispenser for moving small quantities of liquid around.

Vehicle markings

The modeller faces a choice between three options: to paint markings by hand, or to use dry prints or wet decals. Most of the major manufacturers supply sets of decals with their kits. For many years now Italeri have produced the finest wet decals. Personally I only use hand painting or dry prints. Wet prints need very careful application, with additional disciplines, otherwise a perfectly finished vehicle can be spoiled in this final finishing stage. There are four main suppliers of dry prints: *Accurate Armour, Azimut/ADV, Letraset* and *Verlinden*. Accurate Armour also produce a range of borderless water-slide decals, which may be the answer to the nightmare of "silvered" decals often suffered by the modeller. Virtually all normal commercial decals have a clear border; if they are applied to a high gloss surface the transparent border becomes invisible, but on non-gloss finishes this border becomes "silvered" as light is refracted under the decal - which cannot snuggle down tight to such surfaces. Decals also have a multitude of angles to contend with, and the normal decal-

Below

After the primer has cured the model is given its base coat in green Hannants enamel. The dark yellow camouflage is going to be added using Tamiya acrylic (lightened), while the brown element will again be Hannants.

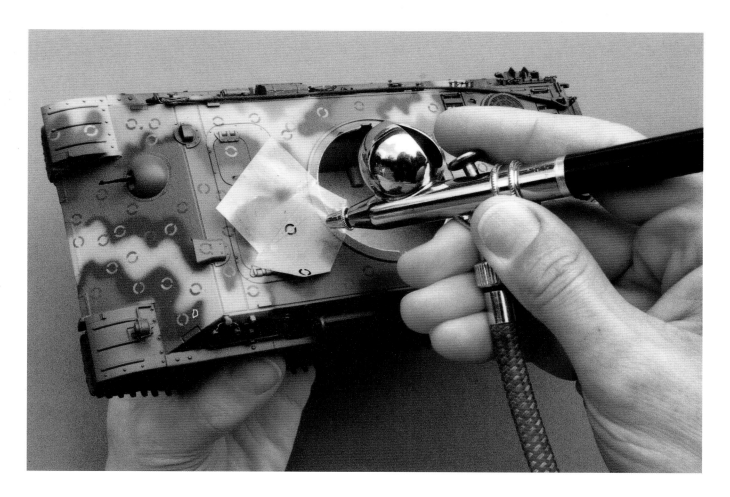

assisting liquids can have a negative effect on acrylic-finished models.

For all these reasons I opted years ago for either dry rub-down prints or hand painting. Dry prints are not without their own problems: they have a limited shelf life, becoming increasing difficult to remove from their mounting sheet after some years, and - their main problem - if they include more than one colour they often suffer from less than perfect registration during the printing process. Some manufacturers adopt no more than two colours per item to mitigate this problem. Others, like *Azimut/ADV*, are more adventurous and generally successful with a superb range of German prints. I am unable to confirm whether *Letraset* still produce their range of four sheets for the ground forces. *Verlinden* products are also excellent value; their dry prints are probably the easiest to remove on the market. Buying dry prints by mail order must always carry the risk of receiving a set that are not perfectly registered; however, all of these main suppliers will gladly exchange imperfect goods.

PAINTING & FINISHING TECHNIQUES

The first step after completion of construction is to thoroughly wash your model. Some scratch-builds and heavy conversions may have taken many months to complete and will therefore have accumulated grease, grit and dust. Even plastic and resin kits built straight from the box have a release agent to

separate them from the moulds. All these impurities will inhibit the tenacity of the primer or paint. I use ordinary household washing liquid, diluted with warm water, and a depleted flat sable. Wash the model very carefully so as not to damage fragile detail; rinse thoroughly with clean cold water; and allow 24 hours to dry - one of the best places to dry/cure models is in the dry warmth of an airing cupboard.

Priming

It is exceptional for me to build straight from the box without additional detail, and my frequent use of brass, aluminium, steel and lead makes it essential that I prime my models. As described above I use automotive acrylic metal primer. There are no special techniques; follow the instructions and shake the can for at least two minutes, or you may spray on large droplets of insufficiently mixed primer. I normally wear a protective glove while I hold the vehicle; if it is a tank, then remove the turret and spray it separately. The spraying movement should run parallel to the axis of the model; depress the trigger before you reach the model and release after you have left it - never start spraying by pointing the nozzle straight at the model, as this can lead to a heavy drenching of primer. This particular type of primer is instantly touch dry, so several light coats can be given. The model should be rotated and sprayed from several directions, the light covering per coat preventing the swamping of fine detail. Another advantage of this primer is that it

Above
The following day, after the paint had cured, I made up some small circular templates to recreate this late-war pattern. Slightly tedious, as it requires three paint changes in the airbrush, the effect is nonetheless striking. The material used is masking film; the punch and die set provided the means to form the circular templates.

also shrinks as it cures, further protecting your detail. I use either white or light grey colour. Other than Schwarzgrau, all German base paints were rather light; should your model have a dark plastic or resin finish, then without a pale primer many finishing coats will be needed to give the correct tonal value to the base colour.

Primers provide the ideal base for subsequent finishing coats. Like all paints they require an adequate curing period; a minimum of 24 hours is recommended - the solvents within the primer must be allowed to evaporate. If you start applying finishing coats before this process is complete then a "vapour trap" may occur, with solvents trapped between the primer and the top coat, causing the latter to degrade and lose its adhesion. Primer may also highlight poor finishes, i.e. seam lines that you thought were invisible before priming. Carry out any corrections at this stage and reprime if necessary. Once you are satisfied with the condition of your primed vehicle you are ready for the final make-or-break phase of a project in which you may have invested many

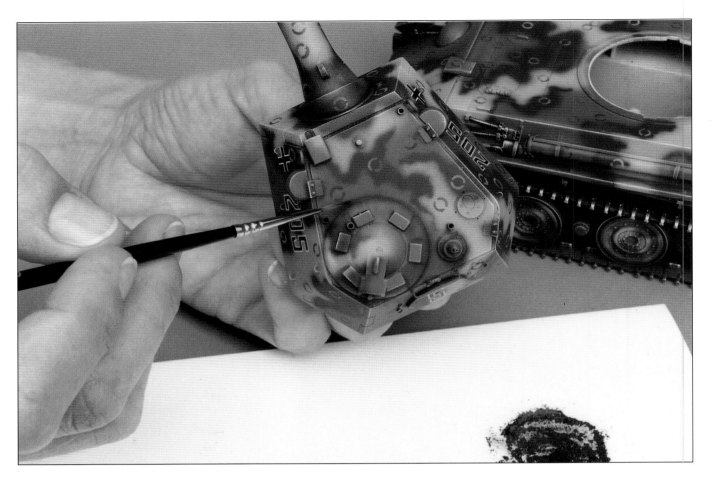

Above

After dry-brushing, the vehicle is ready for the final weathering effect. Black and dark earth pastel chalks are ground to a fine dust. Three separate piles are kept: one black, one dark earth and one a mix of the two. I use a No.0 or 00 sable brush to apply the chalks, and a flat Premier sable to blend. All recessed detail, and the bases of all raised detail, are "painted" with the chalks. Paint them on; blow away any excess; and blend the remainder.

weeks: the finishing paint scheme.

Earlier in this book I mentioned how I planned the camouflage of the vehicle either before I started on the model or during the process of construction. Try to understand what your vehicle will look like once you have completed the camouflage painting. To sit at a table with your model in one hand and an airbrush in the other with no idea of the paint finish is a recipe for disappointment. Photocopy plans and elevations of the vehicle and spend an evening with colouring crayons deciding on a scheme that pleases you. This is the only stage of modelling which really cannot be taught, and for which you may need a little artistic flair to maximise the appearance of your model. The exact application of German camouflage was generally left to the imagination of the individual tank commander and therefore, within reason, anything goes. If you consider that you lack imagination or confidence, then rely on combat photographs for your inspiration.

Painting: acrylics or enamels?

The Tamiya Dark Yellow (XF-60) is a very good match for the actual colour. I firmly recommend the use of acrylics in airbrushes; they are far more user-friendly than enamels, and provided I can get a good match to RAL colours I always use this medium. However, as basic out-of-the-pot colours the modeller is restricted to this Dark Yellow, J.A.Green (XF-13) and Flat Brown (XF-10) for really close matches to the RAL colours.

Historically, RAL 6003 (Olivgrün), 8017 (Braune) and 8002 (Signalbraun) were supplied in five-kilo tins of paste concentrate for dilution by the tank crews. Dilution could be achieved with water, oil, petrol, etc., and final intensity of colour depended upon the extent of this dilution. RAL 6003 (Olivgrün) could appear almost black if undiluted, or a light pea green if heavily treated. It must also be remembered that all colours in both the Tamiya and Hannants ranges are based on a 1:1 scale, i.e. real size, and you must lighten for scale effect. I tend only to lighten the base colour, not the camouflage colours. I would add approximately 25% white to the Dunkelgelb. Schwarzgrau (RAL 7021), commonly referred to as Panzer Grey, will be extensively lightened by the dry-brushing technique and therefore does not need to be lightened by dilution at this stage.

Three basic colour schemes were used in the European theatre of operations: Schwarzgrau, Dunkelgelb, and winter camouflage. Those used in North Africa can be treated in a similar manner to the Dunkelgelb technique. Schwarzgrau was used up to February 1943

and Dunkelgelb from then until the war's end. Throughout the war a white camouflage was applied to vehicles during the winter months (when supplies were adequate). Obviously old supplies were not thrown away, but continued to be used up. Towards the war's end regulations concerning the application broke down and vehicles frequently left the factories in red-brown primer, to which other basic colours were added. I have already mentioned my scepticism about the colour interpretation from black-and-white photographs; and this applies in particular to this late war period, when recent literature tells us that vehicles were to be seen in base Olivgrün camouflaged with some of the other colours and even Schwarzgrau. I have unfortunately no personal research information to confirm these statements. I will describe how I deal with the three basic schemes individually. I should add that the vehicles are complete when I commence painting; tools, ropes, and miscellaneous detail are all in place ready for painting. The single exception to this may be self-propelled anti-tank/artillery vehicles, which will almost certainly be in various sub-assemblies for ease of painting.

Assemble all your materials and tools within easy arm's reach. Your model at this stage should be placed well away from the paints, thinners, etc. - accidents frequently happen. The first step is to pre-set your airbrush; the manufacturer's instructions will describe how it should be reset following previous stripping and cleaning. Minor adjustments can be made once the brush is primed with paint. The next step is to prepare the paint. During storage all paint separates; it is vital that the pigment and medium are thoroughly mixed - more problems occur during both hand- and airbrushing through poorly mixed paint than for any other reason. The paint should be mechanically mixed; stirring the pot with a cocktail stick for twenty seconds does not qualify! Make up a simple L-shaped paddle out of brass rod, approximately 1mm-2mm diameter, ensuring that the diameter will fit in your motor tool collet. Turn the control to the very slowest speed; insert the paddle into the paint pot, and turn the motor on. Do NOT start the motor before insertion - this will only spread the paint around the workbench and walls.... After mixing for approximately one minute, increase the speed somewhat - it is not necessary to use a fast speed. Move the paddle around in the paint, raise and lower it, but never remove it from the paint while the drill is in motion. Its appearance will tell you when the paint is properly mixed: once it is of an even colour and consistency it is ready for use.

Switch the compressor on and set the correct pressure. Once again, airbrushes need different pressure settings for optimum use. For general spraying I use 25 psi (1.75 bar) air pressure. The Aztec type airbrush needs about 30 psi (2.1 bar). Use a large brush (about No.5) to transfer the paint from its container to your mixing palette and add 30% - 40% thinners; I use an eye dropper to transfer the thinners to the palette. For both enamels and acrylics I adopt the same mixing ratio. Hannants enamels are already a satin/eggshell finish, while Tamiya's are matt. If I choose Tamiya, I add 20% gloss acrylic

(Tamiya X-22) to the paint mix. Thoroughly mix the paint/varnish with the thinners; the consistency of the mix should resemble milk, not water, nor single cream.

Load the airbrush carefully and practice on a piece of white paper. Make any necessary adjustments to the setting. The first depression of the trigger frequently produces a splatter effect; this is natural - just remember never to start spraying on the vehicle, start off the model and move onto it. At the setting I have suggested you should be about 100mm from the model for general spraying; closer, and you can drench the model with paint; further away, and the solvent can evaporate before it even reaches the model, producing a gritty effect. Both finishes are highly undesirable and difficult to recover; the latter can be mitigated by leaving it for 24 hours and then, with a flat sable, scrubbing gently to remove these detached paint particles.

I treat the painting of all vehicles as two totally separate operations: the superstructure, and the substructure. The superstructure will support the camouflage scheme, while the substructure - i.e. the lower hull, running gear and tracks - will take the majority of the weathering. It is most important to achieve colour sympathy between the two areas so that there are no hard contrasts between the designated superstructure camouflage scheme and the weathered lower hull. I will describe how to paint each of the three basic schemes in order, but the concept of painting the superstructure as one entity and the substructure as another remains common to all.

Dunkelgelb /Olivgrün (RAL 6003)/ Braune (RAL 8017)

Spray painting the base colour has already been described, and you should by this stage have a very clear idea of the ultimate camouflage finish. While the great majority of vehicles bore a camouflage scheme, some remained in their factory applied Dunkelgelb finish - I will return to this basic finish later. Irrespective of whether the basic Dunkelgelb is from Hannants or Tamiya, I use either of these two manufacturers' paints for the green and red-brown oversprays. For fine line work I use acrylics, and for broader bands of colour the enamels. The mixture ratio of paint to thinners is as described above, but I do alter the pressure settings on the compressor. On my compressor most fine line work is done at 15-18 psi (1.2 bar); this is only a rough guide - it is essential to practice on a scrap of paper before starting on the model. Paint mix, pressure settings, atmospheric conditions and room temperature are all factors that can radically affect the performance of the airbrush from day to day. With a lower operating pressure you will need to be closer to the model. The finest line work may require the nozzle to be held only 2mm - 3mm from the model.

Below
No areas are excluded - every part of the vehicle gets the chalk treatment. Here I used a black/dark earth blend for the superstructure, and neat black for the substructure and running gear.

Above
The completed model; a photograph cannot do justice to the pleasing results obtainable with pastel chalks. They have a surprising tenacity, adhering especially well to matt or satin finishes, and will even tolerate a certain amount of handling, though this should be avoided whenever possible.

The spraying of the Dunkelgelb/camouflage should encompass the whole vehicle including the substructure. Once you are content with the basic colour scheme, do not continue trying to improve it a little further - this is a recipe for an over-painted model. Now is the time to stop, put the model safely to one side, and strip and clean the airbrush. This is where the cellulose thinners is indispensable; it is the only solvent that will totally clean all paint and varnish residues from the brush. (I have already mentioned the precautions that MUST be taken if this potentially lethal solvent is used.)

Depending upon whether the finish is acrylic or enamels, you will decide whether you can immediately proceed to the next step or must wait while the paint cures. By switching mediums it is possible to continue working without interruption. If your model was painted with acrylics, then by using enamels, which employ white spirit as the medium, you are able to proceed immediately. However, if enamels were used for the colour scheme then a minimum of 48 hours should be allowed before applying oil/enamel washes.

Washes of very thinned dark colours help give depth and shadows to your model. They are not essential, however; it is only on Zimmerit finish that I always apply them. If the Zimmerit was correctly applied - so that the "trenches are open at the top", as it were - then the recesses will hold the dark wash, thereby giving greater depth to the finish. I tend to apply washes locally on most other models. For these washes I use Humbrol's high quality thinners with Sepia Extra oil paint, whose sooty, brown/black appearance is ideal. The mixing ratio is about 20% oil paint to thinners, but I do vary this according to locality. If the wash will not capillary, then the mix is too strong and must be weakened. For Zimmerit or large areas I use a No.5 sable, for localised areas a No.0 sable. The model should be held in its correct finished position, i.e. tracks at the bottom - the wash needs to run in the right direction. Once this operation is complete, the thinners must be allowed to evaporate and the oils to dry; due to the small percentage of oils to thinners this will not take more than 24 hours.

The finish at this stage should be satin/eggshell. Hannants paint gives this finish naturally, while the Tamiya equivalent should have achieved it by virtue of the gloss varnish admixture already described. If you have not got a satin finish by this stage, it is vital that your model receives one. A matt model is a dead model! Even without highlighting or dry-brushing a satin-finished vehicle will look much more realistic. The application of insignia, numerals, etc. should be undertaken at this stage, whether by hand-painting, dry

prints or wet decals (although the actual application is dealt with later in this chapter).

The technique of dry-brushing will accentuate the life already imparted to the model by its overall finish. I invariably use oil paints for **dry-brushing**, although I will readily mix these with enamels. Not only are oils gentler on your flat red sables, but the successful blending of oil colours is far easier. As oil paints can take a considerable time to dry, I do not end up with solid brushes after only a few minutes of dry-brushing. I reserve a number of flat sables, in varying stages of depletion, for dry-brushing. Never, ever, attempt to dry-brush with a sable which has retained thinners in the hairs - previous work will be smeared. If you have a limited number of flat sables for changing colours, then consider cleaning the brush with cellulose thinners. This solvent evaporates within seconds to give a totally dry sable; however, the price is that the cellulose causes a fairly rapid acceleration of hair brittleness on the brush.

Unfortunately I do not know any oil paint manufacturer who produces a Dunkelgelb, so you need to mix your own. I do not have any predetermined proportions but tend to play around with the colours until a reasonable match is achieved; the ratio is of the order of 70% yellow ochre, 29% white and just 1% of Prussian blue (the blue in this mix is amazingly strong - use just a fraction too much and you end up with olive green). Once you have achieved a good colour match, dry-brush the vehicle, i.e. all edges, raised detail, etc. Dry-brushing is just what it says: your

Above
Early production PzKfw VI Ausf E Tiger (a "back-dated" Tamiya late production kit with Model Kasten wheels and tracks), painted overall in factory Dunkelgelb using Hannants enamels, with masked/hand-painted numerals and insignia.

brush should be devoid of all apparent paint - before starting, flick the brush to and fro on a piece of card to remove all heavy deposits. Remember that it is easier to add additional paint than it is to remove any excess. The whole vehicle should be dry-brushed with the exception of the substructure. Add white oils to the mix (keeping some of the first Dunkelgelb mix for the substructure) and recommence dry-brushing, but restricting your attentions to the higher raised detail, edges, etc. Continue adding white to the mix until you are able to use off-white without any apparent hard distinction between colours.

While the oils are drying the substructure can be sprayed. As previously described, I use Humbrol Dark Earth No.29 with 30% matt black added. Due to the coarse pigment of this paint it will readily clog the nozzle of the airbrush. Therefore it is essential to airbrush that detail which requires a degree of finesse. The main area this applies to is the junction between the super- and substructures. There needs to be a subtle gradation from the matt substructure to the satin superstructure. As you airbrush this invisible line, draw the brush back a few centimetres, which will allow some drift onto the superstructure. The substructure should be totally airbrushed, including tracks, drive sprockets, road wheels, etc. Large road wheels, like those found on Tigers and Panthers, should not receive a blanket overspray over previously camouflaged areas; restrict the spray to the edges and rims.

Before cleaning your airbrush for the last time on this model prepare a mix of 50/50 thinners and Sepia Extra and spray the muzzle brake and the vehicle's exhausts; once again, use moderation.

Once the substructure has cured (24 hours) you can start dry-brushing it. Start with the basic Dark Earth enamel. Due to all the nooks and crannies of tank substructures your sables can have a very short life dry-brushing; for the initial stages use old brushes. Add increasing quantities of your Dunkelgelb to the Dark Earth. Once you can dry-brush with Dunkelgelb neat then the substructure (apart from chalks and metallics) is finished. You will find that Humbrol Dark Earth is extremely porous to subsequent coats of differing colours, so that the basic hue of Dark Earth is difficult to alter. The only answer is repetitive dry-brushing with your oils. Attempt to achieve colour sympathy between the sub- and superstructure; if there is a hard distinction between them, then rework until this is removed. The goal is a satin superstructure and a matt substructure with an almost imperceptible graduation of colour and finish on the junction between the two.

Next, dry-brush the contact surfaces of track links, guide horns, sprocket teeth, steel rimmed road wheels, etc. with Hannants Oily Steel (X503). This is the penultimate stage of the painting process. I now revert to painting of detail. This is limited to tools, machine gun barrels, exhausts, in fact any small detail that has the basic camouflage finish. Metal tools are painted matt black and dry-brushed with

Oily Steel. The wooden effect on tool handles, jack blocks etc. is easily recreated. Paint these with Tamiya Dark Yellow; once dry (in minutes), give them a strong wash (75% thinners) of Burnt Sienna. I use any dark rust colour to dry-brush exhausts; remember, rust is totally matt, and any satin or gloss finish to rust stains will look false. Visor blocks are first given a Sepia Extra wash; allow this to cure, then paint the blocks with Tamiya Clear Green (X25). If you do want to risk this rather delicate paint job then use the very fine clear artist's varnish to reproduce a glass effect.

The final stage in the painting process is the application of silver. This essential procedure can make or break your model; too little is far better than too much. Use Tamiya Chrome Silver paint marker as the basis for your dry-brushing medium; this is a wonderfully bright finish. However, restrict your dry-brushing to the most exposed areas, e.g. ice chevrons, tips of sprocket teeth, highest raised detail/tools, etc. By using silver on areas that have already been dry-brushed with Oily Steel you will achieve even greater depth to the surface. Turret edges that would have their paint finish abraded by the crews should also be frugally treated.

The final technique is one which I have developed from being an aid to being an integral part of my finishing operation. This is the use of artist's **pastel chalks** (not to be confused with weathering chalks). The use of artist's chalks enables the modeller to exercise more finishing control, with a greater ease and subtlety of finish, than any other medium. The application of dark pastel chalks gives the model a greater depth and perspective then any other method. If the effect is too severe then its removal can be accomplished with the scrubbing action of a sable brush; conversely, additional quantities of chalk can be added. Despite an apparent frailty they do have amazing powers of adhesion and will tolerate a surprising degree of handling. While I have, as usual, a full range of colours, I only ever use dark earth, black and orange. If the vehicle has a Dunkelgelb scheme then I use a ratio of 50/50 dark earth to black mixed. For Schwarzgrau vehicles I use black only; and for winter camouflages I use all three colours.

With a needle file, grind up the two basic colours of black and dark earth. Mix the two with a No.0 sable, and literally paint every recess and the base of all raised detail. Blow away the surplus chalks. With a No.2 flat sable, blend the chalk into the painted surface. Muzzle brakes, recesses of road wheels etc. can be painted with neat black chalk. Recreate stains with a combination of orange and black. Remember stains are caused by weathering of unprotected items, they do not start from nowhere; make the stains run from bolt holes, etc. As you go

about your daily life, observe rusting cars, or even better, construction plant - this is invariably not very well maintained from a painting viewpoint. All this will provide reference on how and where vehicles weather and deteriorate. The combination of a satin finish and matt shadows and stains creates an authentic and most pleasing finish to your model.

Schwarzgrau (RAL7021)

Schwarzgrau is an excellent scheme on which to practice and learn many of the basic painting skills. For a true rendition of this colour the modeller is restricted to Hannants X800. While this colour is usually described as Panzer Grey or dark grey its tonal values suggest that "blue grey" would be more appropriate. Those who have developed a preference for Tamiya acrylics will need to add 20% Flat Blue (XF-8) to Dark Grey (XF-24). The application of Schwarzgrau requires no particular finesse, and therefore it is just as easy to use the exact colour match of Hannants enamels as to mix up Tamiya shades.

All methods and techniques described above under Dunkelgelb apply to this colour application. The vehicle should be airbrushed in total, both substructure and superstructure. At this juncture the markings should be applied (see below). Mix up an oil paint Schwarzgrau using black, white and Prussian Blue; ensure that you have a good match with the Hannants colour. Once the top coat has cured you can commence dry-brushing. Dry-

The variety of visually distinctive camouflage finishes which can be achieved with different proportions, dilutions and patterns of the basic dark yellow, olive green and brown of the February 1943 regulations is surprisingly wide. These examples show variations applied to *(above)* PzKfw V Ausf D Panther - Cromwell resin kit with Model Kasten tracks and some other super-detailing, painted with Tamiya acrylics; *(above right)* detail, Flammpanzer 38(t) conversion of Italeri Hetzer with The Show Modelling etched set and some super-detailing, painted with Tamiya acrylics; *(below right)* detail, SdKfz 251/9 Ausf D, Tamiya kit with The Show Modelling conversion and super-detailing, painted with Tamiya acrylics. All these models use MB Models insignia dry prints, which are no longer available.

brush the whole vehicle; there will, as intended, be areas that you cannot reach, and this is all part of the technique. Once this is done, add a small amount of white to the mix and recommence dry-brushing, beginning to limit the brushing to the raised detail, edges etc. Repeat as previously described until you can dry-brush with off-white. As the superstructure has been painted in oils the curing period may take a day or two in a warm airing cupboard. Paint the small parts etc. in the manner described previously.

Next, "paint" with chalks, but restricting

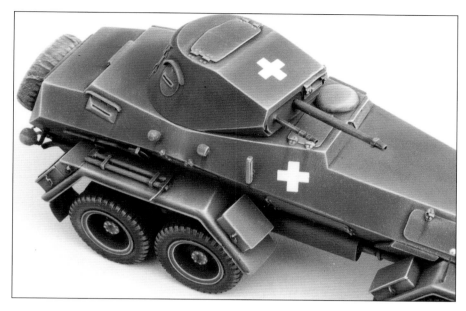

Left

This **PzKfw II Flamm Ausf A und B** *(top)*, made from an Azimut/ADV resin kit, and the **PzKfw III Ausf E** *(below)* made from Sovereign's resin and white metal kit, are both finished with Hannants X-800 Schwarzgrau enamel. The Panzer III, in particular, offers a mass of raised detail for highlighting.

Right and below

Detail, **SdKfz 231 6-Rad** *(right)* from the Sovereign resin kit, painted with Humbrol enamels; and *(below)* Italeri kit of prototype **PzKfw VI Tiger** finished with Hannants enamels, both with markings from Verlinden range of dry prints. Note the "negative" technique of dry-brushing with progressively lighter oils over Schwarzgrau finish.

the colours to black and orange. The orange will represent a slightly rusted effect. All my substructures are treated in an identical way and this scheme is no different; I do, however, tend to substitute white for the Dunkelgelb oils mix when dry-brushing the substructure. After the application of chalks apply any necessary silver as the completion of the model; Schwarzgrau is particularly sympathetic to the subtle use of metallic dry-brushing. A final comment on this scheme is

to remember to achieve the colour sympathy and gradation from the superstructure to the substructure.

Winter camouflage

From the winter of 1941 to the end of the war German forces adopted a winter camouflage over the main approved schemes. This varied depending upon supplies, from the approved whitewash-type paint to chalk, or even white

sheets! While it would be very easy simply to paint your vehicle white with little further work, I much prefer a faded scheme, such as would be found on vehicles in February/March of a new year. Your vehicle type and date will decide whether the base scheme is Schwarzgrau or Dunkelgelb; the technique described here is applicable to either.

This method is almost a "negative" of the standard techniques whereby detail is

highlighted: in this case the detail is darkened to produce perspective. After cleaning, the model should be sprayed with the white acrylic car primer. Twenty-four hours later the vehicle should be given a coat of white matt enamels. Do not consider that because the model already has a white base coat this stage can be omitted. The main painting stage requires the use of oils and they tend to smear on the acrylic finish. With the enamels there is a tendency for some absorption of the oils. Ensure that the enamel is thoroughly cured, then apply a weak wash of the Sepia Extra and thinners. With white camouflage schemes it is essential that the recesses, lines, bolt holes, detail, etc. are accentuated, and this is the easiest way to achieve this. Again, leave to cure.

Mix up in oils your basic Schwarzgrau or Dunkelgelb. Dry-brush the whole of the upper vehicle in white oils. Take a little of your base colour and add to the white oils. Dry-brush raised detail in the usual manner; continue in the "reversed progression", adding increasing quantities of the base colour until you are able to apply it neat without any hard gradations of colour. As the base colour is oils it takes a considerable time for the paint to dry, and you can play around with it until you are satisfied with the result. Blending of oil colours is very easy with a clean, dry, flat sable. Removal of excessive colour can also be undertaken in a similar manner. Remember that the white paint could be washed off with water, and therefore it was common for the base coat to appear from beneath those areas which suffered from

water run-off.

Once the vehicle has completely cured (two days), small details can be painted and a restrained dry-brushing with silver can be applied to raised details and edges. To complete the superstructure use a 50/40 mix of black and dark earth pastel chalks. "Paint" the chalks on as described above; on this scheme I also use orange in recesses to represent a deteriorating paint finish which is showing the first signs of rust; this gives a most pleasing affect. Use black first, then orange to recreate rust and water stains; remember, stains are vertical. The substructure should be treated identically to the Schwarzgrau example, with a greater reliance on pure white as the highlighting medium.

These three schemes cover the basics of my painting techniques; other colours, for example those found in North Africa, used different colours but they are little more than tonal variations on the basic concept. Practice and mastery of these schemes should enable the modeller to undertake any permutation found in use by the wartime German ground forces.

Insignia: decals, dry prints and hand-painting

These are your three options for applying markings to your model. For many years I have used only dry prints or hand-painting, with sometimes a combination of the two. For those who wish to use wet decals there is an additional requirement in the painting

Above
The appearance of a winter-camouflaged front line vehicle like this StuG assault gun calls for a degree of mud application. Here I am using an acrylic car filler mixed with static grass, applied with a hog hair brush. The static grass is best found in railway modelling shops.

Top right
The model has already received a coat of white primer; a subsequent coat of Tamiya white acrylic all over, and a coat of dark earth/black on the substructure only, have been applied with an air-brush.

Bottom right
As the base coat here is water-based acrylic, I was able to apply an immediate dark wash of thinners. Be careful with washes, especially if the base coat is in enamels; ensure total curing of enamels before applying a wash composed of white spirit thinners.

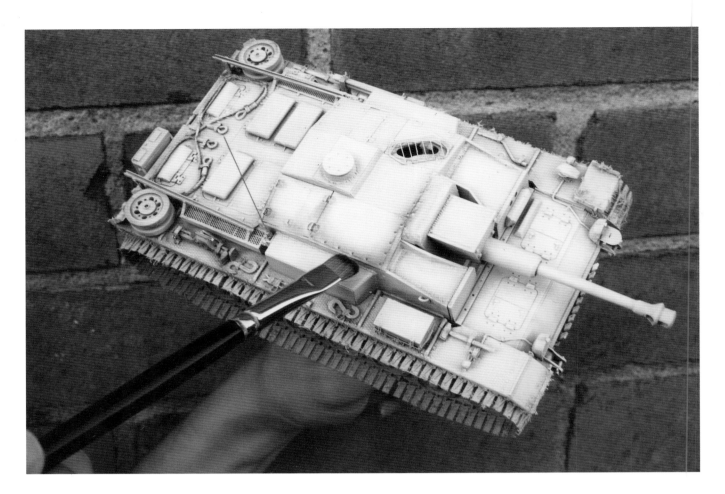

Above left
A Panzer grey oil mix provides the basic colour for dry-brushing. Use only flat red sables for this subtle painting technique; and limit the application to edges, raised detail, etc.

Below left
The StuG model after completion of dry-brushing with Panzer grey - but far from finished yet.

Above
The substructure is resprayed with a very dark earth/black mixture; I allow some "creep" onto the superstructure, especially at the front and rear. The substructure is then dry-brushed with a mixture of dark earth/white oil paint. Continue this process, progressively lightening the mix until neat white can be dry-brushed on without a harsh division being apparent between the paint colours.

Right
Fine detail has been painted, edges have been dry-brushed with metallic steel colours, and a mixture of orange, dark earth and black chalks have been used to weather the vehicle. Now a mixture of alum and white glue is added to recreate snow. The vehicle is meant to represent one seen in the very early spring; not only is the white camouflage consequently faded, but the snow is not fine and powdery but more slushy and heavy as it begins to melt. Note the clamp, for easy handling without constantly touching the finished surfaces. (See Chapter Nine for a photograph of the completed model.)

Above
The application of dry prints is easy provided that they are fresh and you have good access to the location where they are to be fixed. Cut around the dry print leaving sufficient carrier sheet to handle. To rub them down use either a very soft pencil or - preferably - a soft-nosed wooden applicator (the pencil graphite will cover the carrier sheet and you will not be able to see whether all of the print has become detached).

Below
A combination of dry prints and hand-painting, using for clarity in this demonstration a piece of flat plastic rather than a model turret. The numerals are to appear in blue with yellow outlines; so the background - i.e. the turret - should first be sprayed with a flat yellow colour. When this is dry the printed numerals should be carefully applied and only gently pushed down with the finger, not burnished.

sequence. With all wet decals it is imperative that the surface they are to be placed upon is high gloss. This will ensure that no air bubbles are trapped beneath the decal which will refract the light and produce the dreaded silvering. *Accurate Armour* may have come up with a solution in their borderless decals, which to some extent negate the need to gloss varnish the model; we must hope that they will expand their range to incorporate German units. Once traditional decals are applied you will need to spray your vehicle with a satin varnish to reduce the gloss finish. If you do gloss varnish your model, do the complete vehicle, not just the areas where the decal will be applied. It is very easy to give models complete coats of any medium; localised spraying can be difficult.

Due to the irregular surfaces found on many tanks, most modellers will adopt one of the decal-softening products, e.g. the *Micro sol/set solution*. This softens the decal so that it will cling to the compound contours of the model. However, with acrylics this solution can have an adverse effect and deteriorate the paint; so ensure that the gloss varnish used is enamel.

Personally I find dry prints to be the best markings. I do not use any particular manufacturer's products, employing *ADV*, *Verlinden* or *Letraset* prints as required and available. As mentioned earlier, registration remains a problem, but provided you have a good print then the application is normally trouble-free. Dry prints do have a limited shelf life, indicated by the increasing difficulty of removing them from the carrier sheet. Verlindens are probably the easiest to remove, with a good range of prints from divisional and tactical to national emblems.

I use a purpose-made soft nosed wooden pointer to remove the print from the carrier sheet. Do not use a hard pointed object; this will only cause the carrier film to curl and break the print. First cut the print from the main sheet, leaving as much border as possible. Place in position and gently burnish around the edges of the print. Once the print has taken, continue to burnish until it is totally separated. Lift the carrier sheet very carefully; if some of the print is still attached, lay the sheet down again and reburnish. The prints will come with a protective greaseproof cover sheet; cut a small piece of this and place it over the print, burnishing the print through the sheet; this will protect the print while ensuring that it is firmly attached to the model.

If I have reasonably large, solid dry prints for positioning in difficult or delicate locations, e.g. vehicle registration plates, I adopt a slightly different approach. Purchase clear (wet) decal film and apply the dry print to this. Cut the print from the sheet and immerse in water. Once the dry print becomes detached from the carrier film slide the print into position, remembering to wet the area to receive the print. Treat in the way that you would a wet decal: water the print if you need to reposition it, and once satisfied use an absorbent paper towel to remove all water. Gently dab the print, and it will be permanently attached to the model. Do not try this technique on flimsy prints.

If small, isolated lines of dry prints have not taken, infill these with white oils; the narrowest of lines can be painted with this medium. Many of the vehicles in my collection are now over ten years of age, but to date I have not suffered any lifting of the dry prints.

The only permutation on dry prints is a combination of hand-painting and prints. This process needs a little forward planning. Most German vehicles had turret numerals outlined in a colour, usually white. If your model is to have white-outlined numbers then after completion of construction paint the turret white; if you use white automotive acrylic primer then the finish is already available. Apply solid numerals (black is preferable). Do not burnish the dry print, just push it down with your finger, so that subsequent paint camouflage schemes will not creep under the edges. Spray the vehicle as previously described; and while the paint is still soft, within a few hours of application, remove the surplus paint over the dry print with low adhesion tape - insulation tape is ideal. Gently stab the area of paint over the masked numerals; the tape will remove both the paint and the dry print. Be patient; if the tape adhesive is too strong you may also remove some of the paint camouflage, and this will be very difficult to correct.

You should now have perfect solid white numerals; proceed to hand-paint the centres of these in whatever colour you decide, generally black or red. I use *Chroma* colours for their strength and vibrancy. You will almost certainly need to repaint or touch up these numerals several times before you are satisfied.

This technique of mask and strip can be used for a variety of purposes. Low-tack masking film is also very useful for white air recognition bands, which are easily recreated with a little planning. At white primer stage cut out a rectangular patch of film and apply to the model; remove it later after the painting stage, to give a perfect white band for weathering.

The final means of painting signs, numerals etc. is by hand. With Zimmerit-coated vehicles you have little choice. Simply mark out with two parallel lines of insulating tape the maximum depth of the numerals. Hand-paint them in white, and fill in with red or black using *Chroma* colours.

Ground weathering

As stated already, my "three-dimensional" weathering is restricted to the bare minimum, though I do accept that to the diorama modeller this is a more important consideration. Obviously, the weathering colour of the tank substructure must be in sympathy with the ground colour of the diorama to be convincing.

If I have decided to apply some ground effects then I use only two materials: acrylic car filler and static grass - this last can readily be found in model railway hobby shops. The priming and painting of the vehicle should be completed as described above, making no concessions just because the surfaces may now be partially obscured by mud. The application of the mud should be undertaken after completion of the model, including washing and cleaning. My single hog haired bristle brush is used for the application of the filler and static grass. Close study of wartime photographs is essential if you are to put the mud in the right place; for example, heavy applications on the teeth of the drive sprocket

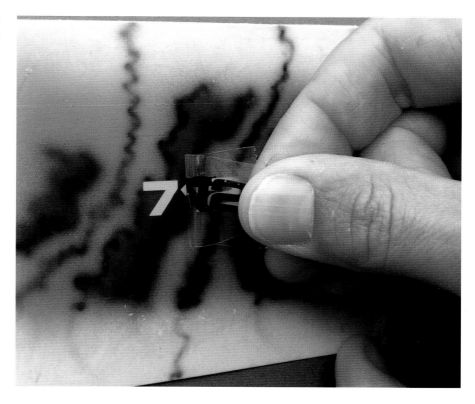

Above
This area of the model should now be air-brushed in the normal way with whatever camouflage scheme is desired; and when this is dry enough not to lift, use tape to catch and remove the dry prints (I usually reduce the stickiness of the tape first by pressing the contact side onto a finger, but trial and error will show what is needed to remove the prints).

Below
Hand-painting the centres of the numerals. I use Chroma colours, as a single pass with this strong medium usually gives sufficient opacity.

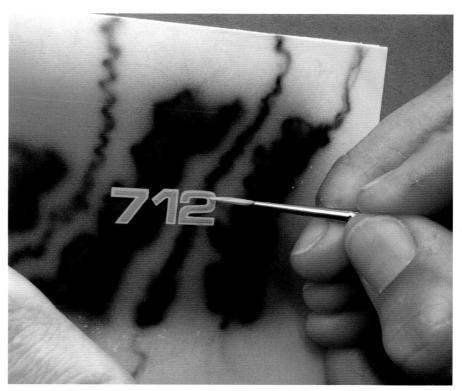

Above

On Zimmerit you have no choice but to hand-paint the numerals - just as the crews of the real vehicles did. Here two strips of low contact insulating tape provide the painting limits for the numerals. Outline the number first before filling the white in.

Below

Infill with scarlet red, touching up the white outline later if necessary. On Zimmerit the numerals need not be perfect - study actual wartime photographs if you need reassurance! As this operation is completed immediately after the model has been sprayed, the numerals will also receive any necessary weathering along with the rest of the tank.

would be ridiculous. Remember that running surfaces shed mud, not collect it, and the displaced mud is often deposited in adjacent areas; again, take any chance to study a modern tank or - more often accessible - a heavy tracked construction vehicle on a muddy site, and note the exact behaviour of thrown-up spoil. The inclusion of the static grass strands in the mud is very important as this is an excellent material to enhance dry-brushing. Even with standard dry-brushing techniques, individual blades of grass can be highlighted.

Air recognition flags

The technique I use for these is both fast and simple. I use industrial two-ply paper hand towels as the basic material. The most important element is *Elmer's* glue, which even after drying is able to reconstitute itself if re-wetted. Mix the glue with water and paint an area of approximately 50mm x 50mm. Use a hairdryer to accelerate the drying process. Once dry, the paper will be stiff and also transparent. Using a template provided with the Tamiya SdKfz 222 kit, I place the paper over the template and paint the flag pattern with gouache colours. Use the dryer again; then cut to size. On the underside of the flag gently dampen the paper until it becomes soft and pliable. Carefully place the flag in position. Remember the paint is once again wet, so avoid smearing the red into the white. Push plenty of creases into the flag; use the dryer once more; and retouch the painting if necessary. When completely dry, use black chalk dust in the bottom of creases to pick out the material texture and provide depth to the flag.

CHAPTER EIGHT
CREW FIGURES

There is no doubt that the inclusion of one or more skillfully finished figures with an armoured vehicle or softskin model adds enormously to its appeal. This is a separate art form, however; and apart from occasional forays into this demanding discipline my vehicle models are generally devoid of figures. I have no hesitation in proposing **Stefan Müller-Herdemertens** as the best painter of World War II figures in 1:35/54mm scale currently exhibiting. I am sure that readers will share my personal gratitude for his contribution of the following notes on his methods; my only regret is the unavoidable brevity of this chapter:

Figure selection

"Man is the measure of all things": you can complete your AFV model to the very highest standard possible, but only the inclusion of an appropriate figure to give human scale provides an accurate visual impression of its dimensions and proportions. In addition to this immediate scale effect, figures also bring "life" to your models - AFVs are not passive, static items but moving, working machines which are part of a soldier's life. Adding a figure reminds us of its purpose and its historical context.

The notes which follow are intended not only to introduce the purist "bare AFV" modeller to the subject, but also to give the diorama modeller who is already familiar with this aspect some suggestions for improving the appearance of his work.

The first task - interesting, but sometimes difficult - is the selection of suitable figures by reviewing the available models in the appropriate scale. This selection should satisfy several criteria. The most immediate is the "visual purpose" of the figure, i.e. selection of a figure wearing a uniform appropriate to the AFV type, theatre and period, and in a physical pose which bears a realistic relationship to the vehicle. These choices demand study of a range of good reference material: both a wide selection of wartime "in combat" photographs, which suggest not only the specific uniforms worn but also characteristic, natural poses; and a small collection of "pure" uniform reference books (see Appendix) for essential colour painting detail once you have decided on the branch and unit of your subject AFV. It should be added that a basic familiarity with the uniform and insignia differences of the various branches of service at various periods of the war is an important aid in identifying and dating the subjects of your wartime AFV reference photographs.

Selection also involves choices based on intended use, and quality. You should consider all the advantages and disadvantages of the available models in different materials. Selection of white metal figures can add appreciably to the weight of your model; a single figure may not be significant, but if your diorama requires a number of figures this is a question worth considering. Again, does the quality of the available "stock" figures allow their use without major conversion? Bear in mind that plastic or resin figures are much easier to convert than white metal ones. The clarity and crispness of casting detail - e.g. faces, and small insignia details - should be checked, particularly on resin figures. Are any items of equipment needed, and if so are they included with figures or available as accessories? Finally, of course, you should consider value for money. Once your choice has been made, you can plan the relative arrangement of figures and AFV within your model.

Building the figures

When you finally sit at your workbench holding the figure, you should first check that all parts are present and undamaged. Clean and prepare them with the appropriate tools and materials; then lay out all the kit parts with any additions which you intend to make, e.g. spare head, photo-etched insignia, different arms, added equipment items, etc. Do a "dry run", test-fitting all parts. You

Below
This small 1:35 scale "Zug" is a selection from among the best figures currently on the market. Each pair (back and front rows) illustrates one of the most commonly used types of German wartime AFV crew uniform. From left to right: one-piece coveralls (Hornet Models back, New Connection front); shirtsleeve order (Wolf and Verlinden); reed-green herringbone twill working dress (Tamiya and Warriors); black and/or field grey woollen Panzer/ Panzerjäger/ Sturmartillerie vehicle uniform (Azimut/ADV and The Show Modelling). (Photo Helge Schling)

should then plan the painting process carefully, just as with the AFV itself - which parts can be assembled at once, and which should be left separate for easy access during painting?

The assembly should then be undertaken, using glues appropriate to the materials you are using. There is no space or need for a detailed description here of the assembly technique; the same basic rules apply as already covered at length in the chapter on AFV model construction. More ambitious conversions or scratch-builds will require study of books specifically devoted to modelling human beings in miniature; see, for instance, *Bill Horan's Military Modelling Masterclass* in this series.

Left
The Hornet figure in the process of slight conversion. The pose has been changed with a Verlinden spare arm; the cut of the uniform, by adding a jacket skirt from plasticard and Duro putty, and a belt buckle from The Show Modelling; and he has been given an Armour Accessories felling axe.

Below
The three stages of head/face painting.
(Left) The head of the New Connection figure, primed only, with Testors enamels.
(Centre) The Hornet spare head at the "shadowed" stage. Note that the details of the face and the cap are painted before the shadowing is undertaken - such definition at this early stage helps establish exactly where to place shadows and highlights.
(Right) The Tamiya head is finished, including highlighting. Note the pale skin tone (done simply with pure white), the "heated" reddish cheeks (this man is working hard...), and the strong overnight beard shadow. The faded sidecap was primed with dark olive Humbrol enamel, and then given a wash of thinned black artist's oil paint; shadows were added in pure black, and highlights in warm grey (which is in fact a beige).

When the figure is assembled, the gaps filled, possible conversion work completed, and all details added or reworked as necessary, you should check the figure with care not only before but also after applying the first primer coat. You may have overlooked some unwanted detail or small error, especially when you have been making use of various parts in different materials and colours, and the primed appearance of the model should make these stand out.

Figure painting

Although readers should be able to follow the painting process through the photographs and captions in this chapter, a few general points should be made. The key element in my painting style is the combination of colour shades of the enamel priming (Humbrol, Testors, etc.) with later washes of artist's oils to obtain the final desired colours. The accompanying photographs and captions detail the most thorough method of painting; but if you prefer a less time-consuming method, you can simply omit the highlighting stage, as I did with the uniforms and equipment of the crew of the Bergepanzer 38(t) Hetzer model illustrated on pages 78 & 88. You can obtain a good effect simply by shadowing the clothing, without additional highlighting.

I hope readers find this brief illustrated "crash course" on my figure painting technique useful; and that it may motivate the hesitant to include this attractive and valuable feature when next modelling an armoured fighting vehicle.

The Tamiya figure wearing reed-green twill working dress (which comes with the Sturmtiger kit) in the process of painting, and demonstrating the key element of Stefan Müller-Herdemertens' technique - priming with carefully chosen enamel colours, then washing with equally carefully chosen shades of artist's oils. The large leg pocket (compare with jacket pocket) still shows the priming coat only - on this figure, Humbrol Light Sea Grey. Both legs have just received the first wash with artist's oils - here, greenish umber from Schminke's Mussini range, which is in fact an olive shade. The whole upper body is already shadowed, again with greenish umber, but this time from the Talens Rembrandt range, because this is a darker shade of bluish dark green. Note that the details and seams are painted in after the first wash, but before the shadowing stage. The crisply sculptured hands are Verlinden spares, with which the originals were replaced simply to comply with the category requirements in a future modelling competition.

The Hornet figure during painting; the original one-piece coverall has been converted to represent a two-piece uniform in commandeered Italian Army camouflage material, often used by Wehrmacht armour crews from 1943 onwards. On his left leg the progress of camouflage painting can be followed. The uniform is completely primed with Testor's sand-coloured enamel; the camouflage pattern is added with artist's oils. The green areas are painted first, then the red-brown, and finally the yellow ochre spots. His right leg shows the completed camouflage pattern. On his right upper body the seams have been added with sepia oil colour; his left upper body is already shadowed, again with sepia. (Photo Helge Schling)

The Tamiya figure completely painted. It has now been shadowed all over with Talens Rembrandt greenish umber oil colour; and the appropriate creases of the clothing have been highlighted with warm grey from the Schmincke Mussini range. The subtle highlighting takes time; but it brings out the many small creases which are only found on clothing of cotton or linen fabrics, and thus emphasises the specific appearance of the herringbone twill. Note the worn appearance of the boots; these were primed with Humbrol Brown Bess, then washed with thinned black artist's oil, and finally highlighted with warm grey - the method SMH always uses for black leather items.(Photo Pazatka/Schneider)

Left
The Hornet figure completely painted, but by the less time-consuming method. This consists of both shadowing and highlighting the complete head, while the hands, camouflage uniform and belt are shadowed only. The boots are primed with Brown Bess enamel and washed with black oil colour; the axe is simply shadowed with sepia and black oils.
(Photo Pazatka/Schneider)

Opposite
A New Connection figure completely painted and mounted, representing the Waffen-SS first issue one-piece coverall in "oakleaf/plane tree" camouflage and camouflaged field cap. The system of priming with enamels and painting the camouflage with oils is similar to that used for the Hornet figure, although with different colours. On this figure the camouflage material is fully highlighted with warm grey, which produces a good faded and worn effect.

Below
New Connection figures made and painted by SMH - by the "time-saving" method, without highlighting - provide a crew for the author's Bergepanzer 38(t) model.

Left and below
SMH's Waffen-SS figure (which won an award at EuroMilitaire 1995) placed with the author's Sturmmörser Tiger and Bergepanther models; note the sense of scale and life produced by including a figure.

CHAPTER NINE
THE COLLECTION

Within a few years of resuming modelling my collection soared to over 100 models. As my ability improved I realised that these early models needed to be replaced with improved versions. To date this process continues, with approximately eight new vehicles added to my collection every year of which perhaps five are replacements. Apart from the Tiger series, I find it very difficult to motivate myself to build repeat versions of models if the original is of an acceptable standard. Once a year almost my entire collection of vehicles is put on display at the international EuroMilitaire show, held in Folkestone during late September. This is my only forum for display, other than magazine articles.

The selection of models illustrated in this chapter represent either difficult-to-make subjects, or vehicles that have special appeal. Where appropriate I have included the briefest notes to enable the modeller to follow the same lines of construction. Regrettably I did not always photograph models just prior to priming/painting; where I have such photographs they are included.

Above and below
Panzerkampfwagen I Ausf F - Cromwell's resin model virtually straight from the box, with MV Products headlights added. Finished in Tamiya acrylics, with Letraset/Verlinden dry prints.

Left and centre
**4.7cm PaK(t) auf PzKfw I Ausf B -
Azimut/ADV resin kit with considerable
super-detailing; stowage etc. on rear deck
from spares box. Finished in Hannants
enamels, faded effect dry-brushed with oils.
Azimut/ADV dry prints, hand-painted
tactical signs.**

Left
**Panzerkampfwagen II Flamm Ausf A u.B -
Azimut/ADV resin model for which I made
the master some years ago, straight from the
box with MV Products headlights. Finished in
Hannants enamels; air recognition bar
produced by masking.**

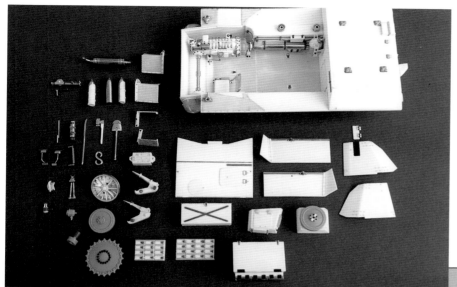

15cm sIG33 auf Fahrgestell PzKfw II(Sf) - scratch-built. The assembled but unpainted model is my first (with a considerable number of errors); the partly assembled layout is the master made for Kirin, not released to date. The painted model is the first version, finished in Humbrol enamels with dry-brushing in oils.

Above
PzKfw II Ausf L - Accurate Armour's first 1:35 kit, built straight from the box with no additions. This kit is old, but still very good, with several refinements since its introduction. Finished in Compucolour enamels (no longer produced) with Verlinden dry prints.

Left and opposite
Panzerjäger 38(t) für 7.62cm PaK36(r) - conversion from Italeri's old 38(t) kit; main ingredients made from plastic, brass and lead, barrel turned on a lathe. Tamiya acrylic Panzer grey (note lack of blue in shade) with Letraset and Verlinden dry prints.

Left
**Panzerjäger 38(t) mit 7.5cm PaK40/3 -
extensive conversion from old Italeri kit.
Finished in Humbrol enamels; note lack of
satin finish and consequent rather dead
appearance. Several coats of varnish had no
effect.**

Right
**Aufklärer auf Fahrgestell PzKfw 38(t) mit
2cm KwK38 - another simple conversion
using an old Italeri kit and part of Tamiya's
2cm KwK38; Compucolour enamels with
Verlinden dry prints.**

Left and below
**Flammpanzer 38(t) - conversion of old Italeri
Hetzer kit, with The Show Modelling etched
set and some super-detailing. Finished in
Tamiya acrylics with MB Models dry prints
(no longer made).**

Right

Bergepanzer 38(t) Hetzer - Dragon's Hetzer kit with The Show Modelling etched set, Scratchyard/New Connection conversion and figures, the latter made and painted by Stefan Müller-Herdemertens (see Chapter Eight). Finished in Tamiya acrylics with Azimut/ADV dry prints. Note, on skirt armour edges, static grass used for weathering (see Chapter Seven).

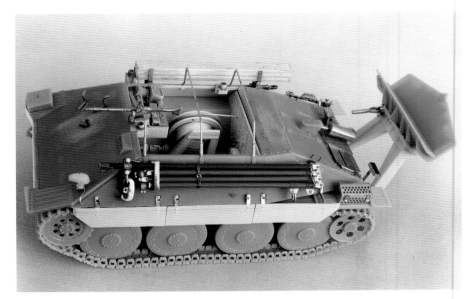

Ardelt 8.8cm PaK43/3 Waffenträger -
Azimut/ADV resin model, for which I made
the master chassis; the gun is an old Azimut
kit with some super-detailing. Finished in
white primer with overspray of Hannants
enamels.

Right
Panzerkampfwagen III Ausf E - Sovereign resin and white metal kit, virtually straight from box; Hannants enamels with Verlinden dry prints, yellow central crosses hand-painted.

Left and below
Panzerkampfwagen III Ausf J (early) - Gunze Sangyo "high tech" kit with considerable super-detailing; Compucolour enamels with Letraset dry prints.

Opposite
7.5cm Sturmgeschütz 40 Ausf F - Dragon kit with Cromwell Ostketten, The Show Modelling etched set, and some additional super-detailing. Finished in Tamiya white acrylic dry-brushed with oils; alum powder for snow effect.

7.5cm Sturmgeschütz 40 Ausf G - conversion from old Tamiya kit, with extensive super-detailing; Compucolour enamels with Letraset dry prints.

Sturminfanteriegeschütz - Sovereign resin and white metal kit; Tamiya acrylics with Letraset dry prints.

Panzerkampfwagen IV Ausf D - Tamiya's old
kit with some super-detailing; jerrycans by
Italeri, rest of stowage from spares box.
Compucolour enamels, hand-painted
numerals, Verlinden dry prints.

Panzerkampfwagen IV Ausf J - Italeri kit with Azimut/ADV conversion and extensive super-detailing. Hannants enamels with MB Models dry prints.

Leichter Flakpanzer IV (3cm) "Kugelblitz" -
old Italeri kit with scratch-built turret;
Compucolour enamels.

Flakpanzer IV/2cm Vierling - Tamiya kit with
some super-detailing. Note the Zimmerit
texture applied to horizontal surfaces with a
pyrogravure. Compucolour enamels with
Letraset dry prints.

3.7cm FlaK auf Fahrgestell PzKfw IV(Sf) - basically converted, super-detailed Tamiya model with Puchala white metal and brass gun kit. Finished in Tamiya acrylics with Verlinden dry prints.

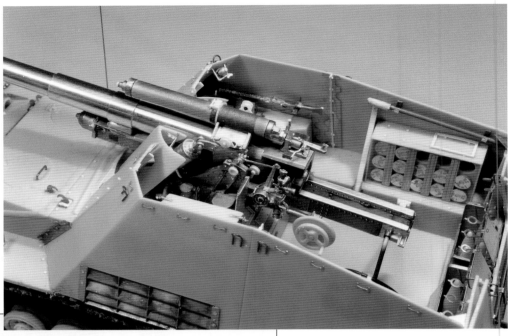

Above left and below
15cm schwere Panzerhaubitze auf Fahrgestell PzKfw III/IV - Dragon kit with considerable conversion and super-detailing; The Show Modelling etched sets; main gun replaced with Gunze Sangyo's 15cm FH18 gun. Finished with Hannants enamels and assorted dry prints.

Above left and below

8.8cm PaK43/1(L/71) auf Fahrgestell PzKfw III/IV(Sf) - old Italeri Panzer IV running gear, Model Kasten tracks, otherwise completely scratch-built. Finished with Humbrol enamels and Letraset dry prints. Note the flat, lifeless finish; many coats of varnish had virtually no effect.

Opposite
Panzerkampfwagen V Ausf D - Cromwell's resin kit with Model Kasten tracks, added side skirts and minor super-detailing. Tamiya acrylics with MB Models dry prints.

Right and below
Panzerkampfwagen V Ausf A - conversion of Tamiya's old Panther kit with scratch-built turret, Milliput Zimmerit, and super-detailing. Finished in Humbrol and Compucolour enamels with hand-painted numerals and crosses.

Below
Jagdpanther - Nichimo's very old kit with Milliput Zimmerit and some super-detailing; Compucolour enamels and hand-painted crosses.

Panzerkampfwagen V Ausf G - Tamiya's new Panther G kit with The Show Modelling etched set, minor conversion and super-detailing. Finished in white acrylic over white primer, dry-brushed with oils and chalks; Azimut/ADV dry prints.

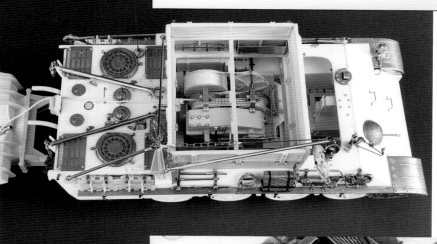

Panzer-Bergegerat Ausf G - master items made for Kirin with intention of releasing full kit with Gunze Sangyo Panther Ausf G, but kit not released to date. Resin items are from the first test shots; many additional items not included in these first shots were remade using brass, plastic, etc. Finished in Tamiya acrylics with Verlinden dry prints.

103

Panzerkampfwagen Panther II - Dragon's kit with scratch-built turret, modified rear deck, The Show Modelling etched set for Panther G, and extensive super-detailing. Hannants enamels with Azimut/ADV dry prints.

E50 - Cromwell resin kit straight from box, apart from MV Products lens in infra-red sighting device. Finished in Tamiya acrylics with masking/hand-painting technique for numerals.

Opposite
Tiger prototype VK4501(P) - Italeri kit with super- detailing, finished in Hannants enamels with Verlinden dry prints.

Right and below
Panzerkampfwagen VI Ausf E (early production) - Tamiya late version converted using Model Kasten "back-dating" set, road wheels and tracks, with etched sets from The Show Modelling and On The Mark, and additional super-detailing. Finished in Hannants enamels with masked/hand-painted numerals and insignia.

Right
Panzerkampfwagen VI Ausf E (mid-production) - Tamiya late version with Model Kasten road wheels and tracks, On The Mark and The Show Modelling etched sets, Milliput Zimmerit, and super-detailing. Tamiya acrylics with hand-painted numerals and crosses.

Left
Panzerkampfwagen VI Ausf E (late production) - Tamiya late version with lead foil side fenders, On The Mark and The Show Modelling etched sets, Milliput Zimmerit, and super-detailing. Finished in white Humbrol enamel with dry-brushed oils, and hand-painted numerals.

Right and below
38cm RW61 auf Sturmmörser Tiger - Tamiya kit, back-dated to Kubinka vehicle, with The Show Modelling etched set. Tamiya acrylics with Azimut/ADV dry prints.

Panzerkampfwagen VI Ausf B (Porsche) - Tamiya kit with The Show Modelling etched set, Milliput Zimmerit, and super-detailing. Finished using both Hannants enamels (green base) and Tamiya acrylics, with hand-painted numerals.

Panzerkampfwagen VI Ausf B (Henschel) - Tamiya model with The Show Modelling etched set, lead foil fenders where battle-damaged, Milliput Zimmerit, and super-detailing. Tamiya acrylics with hand-painted numerals and insignia.

Jagdtiger - combination of old Tamiya and Nichimo kits, with On The Mark etched set, Model Kasten tracks, Milliput Zimmerit, and super-detailing. Tamiya acrylics with Letraset dry prints.

Neubaufahrzeug - Cromwell resin kit, built straight from the box, and finished with Hannants enamels with Verlinden dry prints.

Panzerkampfwagen "Maus" - Dragon kit with improvements and super-detailing; Tamiya acrylics, with masking technique for numerals.

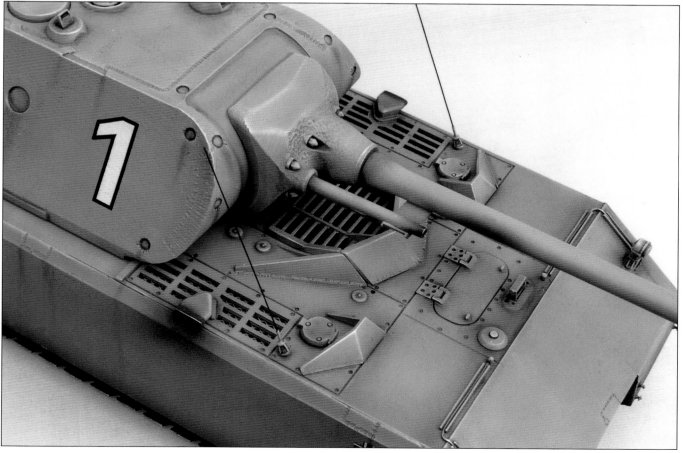

Left and below
Schweres Minenräumer - Armour Accessories resin, white metal and etched brass kit, built straight from the box. Tamiya acrylics with Verlinden dry prints; masking technique for air recognition band.

Below
S gl gep PKW (SdKfz 247) - Sovereign's resin and white metal kit with minor additional detailing. Finished in Hannants enamels with various masking techniques; hand-painted pennants.

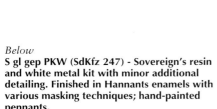

Right
Schwerer Panzerspähwagen (SdKfz 231) 6-Rad - Sovereign's resin kit; Humbrol enamels and Verlinden dry prints.

Left and below
Panzerfunkwagen (SdKfz 263) 8-Rad - converted, super-detailed Tamiya kit, with The Show Modelling etched set. Humbrol enamels, Verlinden dry prints.

Schwerer Panzerspähwagen (2cm) (SdKfz 234/1) - Italeri kit with Azimut/ADV conversion; Humbrol enamels, MB Models dry prints.

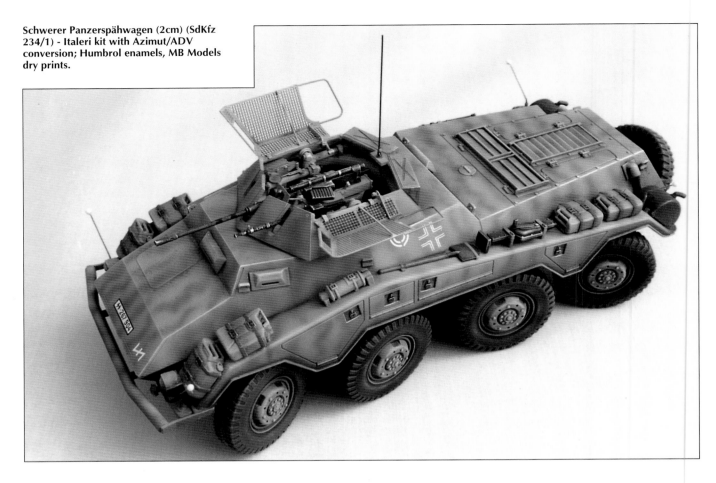

Panzerspähwagen (Fu) Panhard 178-P204(f) - AL.BY injection moulded plastic kit with scratch-built aerial frame and some minor conversion work. Hannants enamels with Verlinden dry prints.

Panzerspähwagen AB41 201(i) - Azimut/ADV resin kit with minor detailing; Hannants enamels, Letraset dry prints.

Mercedes Benz G4 & Zundapp 750 - Azimut/ADV resin Mercedes kit with super-detailing, replacement of some components e.g. windscreen, lights, etc. Italeri Zundapp with The Show Modelling etched set. Finished with Hannants enamels; oil paints for vehicle interior; hand-painted pennants.

Right
**Steyr 1500 - Azimut/ADV resin kit with
super-detailing and additions from the
spares box; Hannants enamels,
Verlinden dry prints.**

Below
**3.7cm FlaK36 auf s gl LKW 4.5t
Bussing Nag - Azimut/ADV Bussing
Nag and Tamiya FlaK; The Show
Modelling FlaK set, but with extensive
correction and super-detailing.
Finished in Tamiya acrylics with
Verlinden dry prints.**

Right
2cm FlaK auf Fahrgestell Zugkraftwagen lt (SdKfz 10/4) - Esci kit with super-detailing and additions from the spares box.

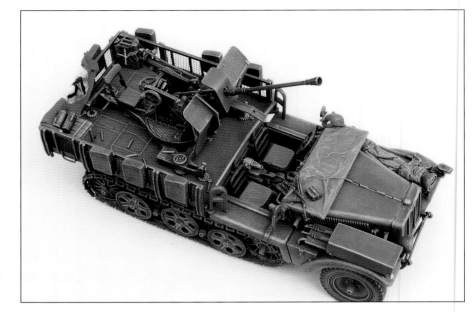

Below
Leichter gepanzerter Munitionskraftwagen (SdKfz 252) - Tamiya model with Peddinghaus conversion (extensively rebuilt), and scratch-built ammunition trailer. Tamiya acrylics with Verlinden dry prints.

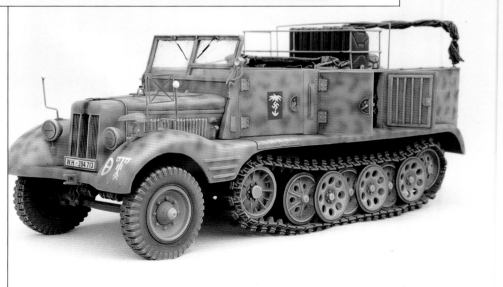

Right
HL kl 6 (SdKfz 11) - Sovereign's resin kit with Model Kasten tracks; Compucolour enamels, Verlinden dry prints.

HL kl 6 3-ton semi-track - Azimut's white
metal kit with stowage material from the
spares box; Tamiya acrylics with Letraset and
Azimut/ADV dry prints.

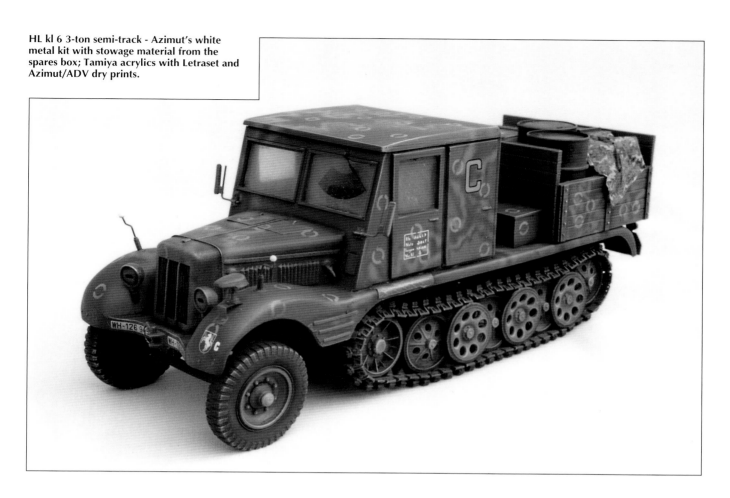

This page
SdKfz 251/20 Ausf D - Tamiya's SdKfz 251 kit with The Show Modelling 60cm searchlight, Model Kasten tracks, remainder scratch-built; infra-red lens is made from solar reflective film used on buildings. The finish is in Tamiya acrylics with MB Models dry prints.

Right
SdKfz 251/9 mittlerer Schützenpanzerwagen Ausf D - Tamiya kit with Verlinden detailing set (poor fitting) and Model Kasten tracks, super-detailed with extras from the spares box. Finished in Tamiya acrylics with masked/hand-painted numerals, MB Models dry prints.

SdKfz 251/9 mittlerer Schützenpanzerwagen Ausf D (late production) - Tamiya model with The Show Modelling conversion kit and some super-detailing. Tamiya acrylics, MB Models dry prints.

15cm Panzerwerfer 42 (Zehnling) auf sWS -
NKC basic kit with scratch-built rear; Werfer
from Azimut's Maultier, for which I made the
master; side stowage panel from The Show
Modelling SdKfz 251 set. Finished in Tamiya
acrylics with Letraset and MB Models dry
prints.

15cm Panzerwerfer 42 (Zehnling) auf sWS -
NKC basic kit with scratch-built rear; Werfer
from Azimut's Maultier, for which I made the
master; side stowage panel from The Show
Modelling SdKfz 251 set. Finished in Tamiya
acrylics with Letraset and MB Models dry
prints.

Land-Wasser-Schlepper - Mini Art Studio's impressive all-resin kit, here with some small parts replaced by brass, nylon cord and finger bandage fenders. Tamiya acrylics, oils, and Verlinden dry prints.

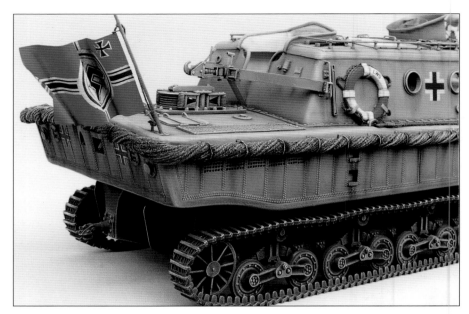

APPENDIX

Listed below, by chapter number, are the names and addresses of manufacturers or (where available) UK distributors or representative suppliers of some of the products mentioned in the text. Where no UK supplier is listed readers are advised to contact the overseas manufacturer's address.

Chapter One: Tools

X-acto hobby knife holders; Swan Morton surgical blades; Milliput epoxy putty - most good hobby shops.
UMV Swiss files; Taxal tweezers; NSD pliers; beading tools; glass fibre cleaning pens; drill tools & accessories - Shesto Ltd., Unit 2, Sapcote Trading Eastate, 374 High Road, Willesden, London NW10 2DH.
Como Drills, Mill House, Mill Lane, Worth, Deal, Kent.
Punch & die set; Pyrogravure - Historex Agents, Wellington House, 157 Snargate Street, Dover, Kent CT17 9BZ.
P-cutter & Compass cutter - ED Models, 64 Stratford Road, Shirley, Solihull, West Midlands B90 3LP.
Chopper & True Sander - Micro Mark, 340-1832 Snyder Avenue, Berkeley Heights, New Jersey 07922-1595, USA.
Elmers Glue-All - Borden Inc., Dep CP, Columbus, Ohio 43215, USA.
Organic vapour respirator Type 4255 - 3M United Kingdom plc, 3M House, Bracknell, Berkshire RG12 1JU.

Chapter Two: Reference Material

Museums (with representative response times to author's enquiries given in brackets):

The Tank Museum
Bovington Camp, nr.Wareham, Dorset BH20 6JG (5 days)
Imperial War Museum
Lambeth Road, London SE1 6HZ (42 days)
Panzermuseum Munster
Hans-Kruger Strasse, BE 33 3042 Munster, Germany (20 days)
Bundesamt für Wehrtechnik u.Beschaffung
Postfach 7360, 56057 Koblenz, Germany (33 days)
Auto u.Technik Museum
Obere Au 2, 74889 Sinsheim, Germany (13 days)
Musée des Blindés (Musée de la Cavalerie)
Hotel du Commandement, 1 Place du Chardonnet, 49409 Saumur Cedex, France (63 days)
Panssarimuseo (Armour Museum)
SF-13700 Paroannummi, Finland (59 days)
US Army Ordnance Museum
Aberdeen Proving Ground, Maryland 21005-5201, USA (18 days)
Patton Museum of Cavalry & Armor
PO Box 208, Fort Knox, Kentucky 40121-0208, USA (20 days)

Reference books

Publishers' addresses are given for overseas publications, but European and US titles should be available in the UK through specialist dealers, e.g. Motorbooks, 33 St Martin's Court, London WV2N 4AL; or Historex Agents, Wellington House, 157 Snargate Street, Dover, Kent CT17 9BZ.

Achtung Panzer series; Panzers in Saumur series; Panzer File 94-95
Dai Nippon Kaiga Co.Ltd., Nishiki-cho 1-7, Kanda Chiyoda-ku, Tokyo 101, Japan (available in UK through Historex Agents; or Brian Sherriff Ltd., PO Box 6950, Forfar DD8 3YF, Scotland)
German World War II Organisational series
Dr.Leo W.G.Niehorster, Aegidiendamm 8, 3000 Hanover 1, Germany
German Armour & Military Vehicle series (Walter J.Spielberger)
Motorbuch Verlag, Postfach 10 37 43, 70032 Stuttgart, Germany
Panzer Colours 1, 2 & 3 (Bruce Culver)
Squadron Signal Publications, 1115 Crowley Drive, Carrollton, Texas 75006, USA; published in UK by Arms & Armour Press, Cassell plc, Villiers House, 41-47 The Strand, London WC2N 5JE
Tigers in Combat (Wolfgang Schneider)
J.J.Fedorowicz Publishing Inc., 106 Browning Blvd., Winnipeg, Manitoba, Canada R3K OL7
Encyclopedia of German Tanks of WWII (Chamberlain & Doyle) Arms & Armour Press - see above

Chapter Three: Available Models

Products of major manufacturers will generally be available in the UK from most good hobby shops; their addresses are given, however, as well as those of smaller manufacturers and those who deal mainly through direct mail order. See above for address of Historex Agents Ltd.

Accurate Armour
Unit 15-16, Kingston Ind.Estate, Port Glasgow, Inverclyde, Scotland PA14 5DG (mail order service)
AL.BY Miniatures
BP 34, F82400 Valence d'Agen, France (mail order service)
Armour Accessories/ Sovereign Models (available through Historex Agents)
Azimut/ADV
8 rue Baulant, 75012 Paris, France (also through Historex Agents)
Cromwell Models
Progress House, 39 Kirkpatrick Street, Glasgow G40 3RZ, Scotland (mail order service)
DES
27 rue des Hauts de Bonneau, 94500 Champigny sur Marne, France (mail order service)

Dragon
603-609 Castle Peak Rd., Kong Nam Ind.Bldg./10th Floor B-1, Tsuen Wan, New Territories, Hong Kong
Gunze Sangyo
Aoba Dailchi Bldg., Kudan-minami 2-3-1, Chiyoda-ku, Tokyo, Japan
H&K35 (NKC)
Mopicom, 104 avenue Pierre Semard, 95400 Villiers la Belle, France (mail order service)
Hecker & Goros
Römerhofweg 51c, 8046 Garching, Germany (also through Historex Agents)
Italeri
1-40012 Calderara di Reno, Italy
Mini Art Studies
Flat 2B Prince Garden, 284 Prince Edward Road West, Kowloon, Hong Kong (mail order service)
Nichimo
Kubo-chu 135, Sano-City, Tochigi 327, Japan
Precision Models
Elf Septenberlaan 24, B-3660 Opglabbeek, Belgium (mail order service)
Puchala Zinnminiaturen
Hildenbrandstrasse 1, Postfach 10, 7906 Blaustein- Herri, Germany (also through Historex Agents)
Scale Model Accessories Ltd.
160 Green Street, Enfield, Middlesex EN3 7LB (mail order service)
Tamiya
Ondawara 3-7, Shizuoka-City, Shizuoka 422, Japan
Verlinden Productions
Ondernemersstraat 4, B-2500 Lier, Belgium (also through Historex Agents)

Chapter Four: Construction & Super-Detailing
Chapter Five: Conversions & Scratch-Building

Clipper Models
c/o Donald, 5-13-15 103 Inokashira, Mitaka, Tokyo 181, Japan (mail order service)
Cornerstone Models
14210 Westchester Drive, Colorado Springs, Colorado 80921, USA (mail order service)
Eduard Model Accessories Co.Ltd.
28 rijna 681, 435 02 Most, Czech Republic (also through Hannants, 29-31 Trafalgar Street, Lowestoft, Suffolk NR32 2AT, UK)
Evergreen Scale Models
Kirkland, Washington 98034, USA
Friulmodellismo
Di Guiseppe Puppato, Via Pazzan 73, 33010 Pagnacco/Udine, Italy (also through Historex Agents)
Grandt Line
1040B Shary Court, Concord, California 94518, USA (also through Historex Agents)
John K.Flack
1 Meadow Bank, Kilmington, Exminster, Devon EX13 7RL (mail order service)

Jordy Rubio
Av.Gaudi 56, 08025 Barcelona, Spain
(also through Brian Sherriff Ltd.-
see under Chapter Two)
Model Kasten
c/o Art Box, Grand P Monaco 3F, Nando-cho
3, Shinjuku-ku, Tokyo 162, Japan (also
through Brian Sherriff Ltd.- see under
Chapter Two)
MV Products
PO Box 6622, Orange, California 92610-
6622, USA (mail order service)
New Connection Models
Dorfgütingen 40, 91555 Feuchtwagen,
Germany (mail order service)
On The Mark
PO Box 663, Louisville, Colorado 80027,
USA (mail order service)
Plastruct
City of Industry, California 91748, USA
Scale Link Ltd.
Rear of Talbot Hotel, Blandford Road,
Iwerne Minster, Dorset DT11 8QN (mail
order service)
The Show Modelling
Baumann, Casa Verde B1- C, 13-12,
Daita 3 Chome, Setagaya-ku, Tokyo 155,
Japan (also through Historex Agents)
Slater's Plastikard
Royal Bank Buildings, Temple Road, Matlock
Bath, Derbyshire DE4 3PG
Sutcliffe Productions
Westcombe, Shepton Mallet, Somerset

Waldron Model Products
PO Box 431, Merlin, Oregon 97532, USA
(contact for local distributor details)

Chapter Six: Specialist Techniques

Carrs Modelling Products
528 Kingston Road, Raynes Park, London
SW20 8DT (mail order service, or through
Shesto Ltd. - see under Chapter One)

Chapter Seven: Painting, Weathering & Finishing

Chromacolour International
11 Grange Mills, Weir Road, London SW12
0NE (mail order service)
Faber Castell GmbH
D-8504 Stein/Nürnberg, Germany
(available in good UK art shops)
A.S.Handover Ltd.
Angle Yard, Highgate High Street, London
N6 5JU (also through Historex Agents)
Hannants
Trafalgar House, 29-31 Trafalgar Street,
Lowestoft, Suffolk NR32 2AT (mail order
service)
Premier sable brushes
Premier Brush Co., 20 Messaline Avenue,
Acton, London W3 6JX (available in good art
shops)

Rembrandt oils & varnishes
Talens, PO Box 4, Apeldoorn, Netherlands
(available in good UK art shops)

Chapter Eight: Crew Figures
Relevant reference books include:

Bill Horan's Military Modelling Masterclass,
Windrow & Greene Ltd., London (1994)
*German Army Uniforms & Insignia 1933-
1945*, Brian L.Davis, Arms & Armour Press
Ltd., London (1971)
*German Army Uniforms of World War II in
Colour Photographs*, Wade Krawczyk,
Windrow & Greene Ltd., London (1996)
*Field Uniforms of German Army Panzer
Forces in World War II*, Michael H.Pruett &
Robert J.Edwards, J.J.Fedorowicz Publishing
Inc., Winnipeg (1993)
*Wehrmacht Camouflage Uniforms & Post-
War Derivatives*, Daniel Peterson, Windrow
& Greene Ltd., London (1995)
Waffen-SS Uniforms in Colour Photographs,
Andrew Steven & Peter Amodio, Windrow &
Greene Ltd., London (1990)
*Waffen-SS Camouflage Uniforms & Post-War
Derivatives*, Daniel Peterson, Windrow &
Greene Ltd., London (1995)
Rommel's Army in Africa, Dal McGuirk,
Century Hutchinson Australia Pty.Ltd.,
Melbourne (1987)